Pioneer Aviator

Terry Gwynn-Jones has published seven books, including *True Australian Air Stories* and *The Air Racers*. He was a consultant and writer for the Time-Life *Epic of Flight* series and in 1987 was appointed to the Board of Advisors of the Smithsonian Institution's National Air and Space Museum History of Aviation book project. Born in Malvern, England, Terry Gwynn-Jones joined the RAF in 1951 and was a pilot in the RAF, the Royal Canadian Air Force, and the RAAF. In 1975 he teamed with Gold Coast pilot Denys Dalton to set a new around-the-world speed record. Presently a pilot with the Department of Aviation, he is based in Brisbane.

Pioneer Aviator

The Remarkable Life of Lores Bonney

Terry Gwynn-Jones

University of Queensland Press
ST LUCIA • LONDON • NEW YORK

First published 1979 by Rigby Limited
Second edition published 1988 by University of Queensland Press
Box 42, St Lucia, Queensland, Australia

Printed in Australia by The Book Printer, Melbourne

Distributed in the UK and Europe by University of Queensland Press
Dunhams Lane, Letchworth, Herts. SG6 1LF England

Distributed in the USA and Canada by University of Queensland Press
250 Commercial Street, Manchester, NH 03101 USA

Cataloguing in Publication Data

National Library of Australia
Gwynn-Jones, Terry, 1933-
Pioneer aviator, the remarkable life of Lores Bonney,
Includes index.
ISBN 0 7022 2118 X.
1. Bonney, Lores 1897- . 2. Air pilots — Australia — Biography. I. Gwynn-Jones, Terry, 1933- . Pioneer airwoman : the story of Mrs Bonney. II. Title. III. Title : Pioneer airwoman : the story of Mrs Bonney.
629.13'092'4

British Library (data available)

Library of Congress (data applied for)

ISBN 0 7022 2118 X

In memory of all those forgotten women pioneers

'We can lift ourselves out of ignorance, we can find ourselves as creatures of excellence and intelligence and skill. We can be free! We can learn to fly!'

Richard Bach in
Jonathan Livingston Seagull

Contents

Acknowledgments

There are a number of people I must thank for their help in preparing this book. The writer of any biography depends on a team of helpers. My team was small but the quality of their assistance made up for their lack of numbers. My thanks to Adrienne Swanton, who produced the ABC television documentary, *'Somehow we almost forgot Mrs Bonney'*. I am indebted to her for the use of her research tapes.

Thanks also to Denys and Norma Dalton whose generous help has added immeasurably to this book. My flight to England with them in 1976 in their Beechcraft Duke provided invaluable background information of the route followed by Mrs Bonney.

For the clue that led me first to Mrs Bonney I must specially thank my friend Col Kelly. His constant enthusiasm and his assistance to all those who attempt to record the history of Australian aviation, should not go unrecorded.

Nor should the work of my son Anthony who spent many long nights photocopying Mrs Bonney's old snapshots to illustrate the book. His insistence on quality regardless of time has produced photographs I am proud to use.

Finally I would like to thank my wife Susan who had to live with me through the hectic trauma of writing this book. Patient to the last she encouraged me, coming up with just the right word at the right time, and finally took on the task of proofreading my atrociously spelt, inadequately punctuated and two-finger-typed copy. Her contribution is reflected throughout the book.

Preface

I first met Mrs Bonney in 1973. At that time I had had several articles on early Australian aviation published and I was on the lookout for a new and, if possible, forgotten subject.

A few weeks earlier I had been researching the flights of Sir Francis Chichester in his de Havilland Moth. For background information I had turned to a technical book on his aircraft. In the section listing the history of these famous aircraft, I came across an entry recording that a DH 60 Gipsy Moth had been sold in 1932 to a Brisbane woman named Mrs Harry Bonney. Next to the listing was the simple statement that she had flown the aircraft solo to England in 1933.

My curiosity was aroused. At that time I was not aware of any Australian woman pilot having made a flight of real historical significance. A solo flight from Australia to England in 1933, whether by a man or a woman, was to my mind, significant indeed.

During the next week or two I asked friends in the aviation business whether they knew of Mrs Bonney. They could all recall the English aviatrix Amy Johnson and her flight to Australia in a DH Moth. They knew that there was a famous New Zealand airwoman, Jean Batten. And, of course, they had all read about the strange disappearance of America's Amelia Earhart. But Mrs Bonney? One or two could remember that there was a woman who 'flew around the area a bit' in the early 1930s. But they were sure she didn't do anything as memorable as flying solo to England. Most simply looked blank and scratched their heads.

Later, I spoke with Col Kelly, an airworthiness surveyor with the Department of Transport. I knew Col had been an apprentice aircraft engineer in Brisbane in the early 1930s. He remembered her.

'She was well known around Archerfield in the old days,' he said. 'She made a number of long flights including one to England and a later one to South Africa, but never obtained the recognition she deserved. Last I heard of her she had retired to the Gold Coast somewhere after her husband died. That was years ago. But I think she is still alive.'

I found a listing for a 'Bonney' in the Gold Coast telephone directory and called the number. An alert female voice answered . . . Yes, she was the Mrs Harry Bonney who flew to England . . . No, she wasn't sure she really wanted to talk about it . . . it was all so long ago . . . Well if it was so important and I wanted to meet her then I should call down for afternoon tea next Sunday.

Before I drove down to her house in Miami, Queensland, I spent several evenings poring over every book on early Australian aviation I could find. Nowhere was she mentioned. Amy Johnson's exploits came up time and again, but all the authors were either ignorant of, or chose to ignore, Mrs Bonney's flights.

When my wife and I arrived at her home we were greeted by a very gracious, but somewhat reserved silver-haired lady, who was obviously puzzled as to why we were there. When she learned that I, too, was a pilot, the curtain of reserve lifted; she fell immediately into a relaxed yet enthusiastic discussion of aeroplanes. Though total strangers, within minutes we were talking like old friends. This ability for instant rapport is, I believe, common among pilots the world over.

I told her I would like to write an article on her flights for the Brisbane *Sunday Mail*. At first she did not seem to want to talk about her own flying experiences. It was so long ago, she said, and she had cut herself off from aviation when she stopped flying. To recall her flights only intensified how much she missed flying.

Afternoon tea was over and we were on to late-afternoon drinks. I must have a second one, she insisted. A bird couldn't fly on only one wing. It was then that she opened a large trunk full of old photographs and clippings, albumn after albumn of them, as well as scrapbooks galore and old log books — it was a treasure trove of the early days of flying in Queensland. I soon learnt that she had made not one, but four record-setting flights. How then, in the short space of forty years, had she apparently been forgotten?

It was not until we had left her home with plans to meet again, and were well on the road back to Brisbane, that the answer came. She had flown in the shadow of Sir Charles Kingsford Smith, Bert Hinkler and the other great Australian pioneer airmen. Australians have always been prepared to make heroes of their men and chronicle their achievements. However, in the early 'thirties women were only just beginning to emerge from the kitchen.

It was time this long-forgotten airwoman received the recognition she so justly deserved. The best way to start the ball rolling, I thought, was to write about her.

During the next four years I was able to publish several short articles on her flying career. In 1975 I was fortunate to meet Laurie Muller, the Queensland manager of Rigby Limited. He was as enthusiastic as I was when told of her achievements. He asked me to write about her in a book of short stories about Australian aviation, *True Australian Air Stories* published in 1977. It generated enough interest for Rigby to publish this biography.

In the meantime, I had also approached Adrienne Swanton, a feature producer with ABC television in Brisbane, who had recently made two fascinating programmes on Bert Hinkler and Bernard O'Reilly of the 1937 Stinson crash fame. She, too, shared my enthusiasm and in 1976 produced an absorbing programme on Mrs Bonney.

During this time I was able to watch a shy, retiring lady in her eightieth year, come out of seclusion and move into aviation circles again. In doing so she seemed twenty years younger. Today I marvel at her zest and love of life. I hardly recognise her as the person I met five years ago. In

1978 during the Kingsford Smith Fiftieth Anniversary celebrations in Brisbane she attended six official functions in the space of twenty-four hours.

I am indebted to her for the days we have spent together recalling her life. Without her enthusiasm, her quite remarkable memory and her humour this book would never have been written.

Following the second World War she sat down and wrote a draft manuscript for a book about her flights with the working title *I wandered the world with a Gipsy*. It was never published. In it she said,

'Writing has clarified for me the rather chaotic memories of a wonderful experience. I wandered in many lands and peered into some strange and little known corners of the earth.

'Flying today is a very different thing from what it was in those days. We take a plane as casually as we take a bus. I would like to think these flights of mine have a small corner in the history of that achievement.'

There is no doubt Mrs Bonney has earned that small corner. No book can fully recapture what this remarkable woman accomplished. To appreciate the hardships and the determination required of the early pioneers in their wood, wire and fabric machines, one would need to have been an unseen passenger crammed somewhere in a corner of their tiny open cockpits.

In 1976, Gold Coast pilot Denys Dalton, myself and our wives, retraced most of Mrs Bonney's route to England in a modern twin-engined light aircraft. We cruised at three times the speed of her old Moth and were able to fly well above the bad weather she had to stagger through. We also had the benefits of air-conditioning, excellent servicing facilities, modern airports and sophisticated radio navigation aids. They didn't exist in Mrs Bonney's day. Her aircraft didn't even carry a radio.

However, though we flew in comparative arm-chair comfort, we were able to see something of what Mrs Bonney and others took on. One day of our flight particularly sticks in my mind. We were half way across the Saudi Arabian desert, with the ground-level temperature more than 40°C, when we were forced to leave our normal smooth and cool cruising level of 7000 metres. Our pressurisation and air-conditioning were 'on the blink' and we were down to 2000 metres over the arid desert. Blowing sand reduced our forward visibility to a couple of kilometres and the aircraft was being belted all over the place by thermal air currents rising from the white-hot desert floor. It was then that I realised the true guts and determination of Mrs Bonney. She did her whole flight at this level. Not only that, she was in an open cockpit, flying about the speed of a small car, with only a compass to find her way across this desert. How on earth did she do it? There is no way in the world I would have tried it.

That flight, plus my own recollection of training in Tiger Moths, direct descendants of her aircraft, made me better understand the magnitude of Mrs Bonney's achievements and her courage. Australians have yet to recognise that they have their own pioneer airwoman, born in the same mould as Johnson, Batten and Earhart.

Somehow we almost forgot Mrs Bonney. I write this book in the hope that another forty years on, Australians will not still be scratching their heads when her name is mentioned.

Terry Gwynn-Jones
Brisbane 1979

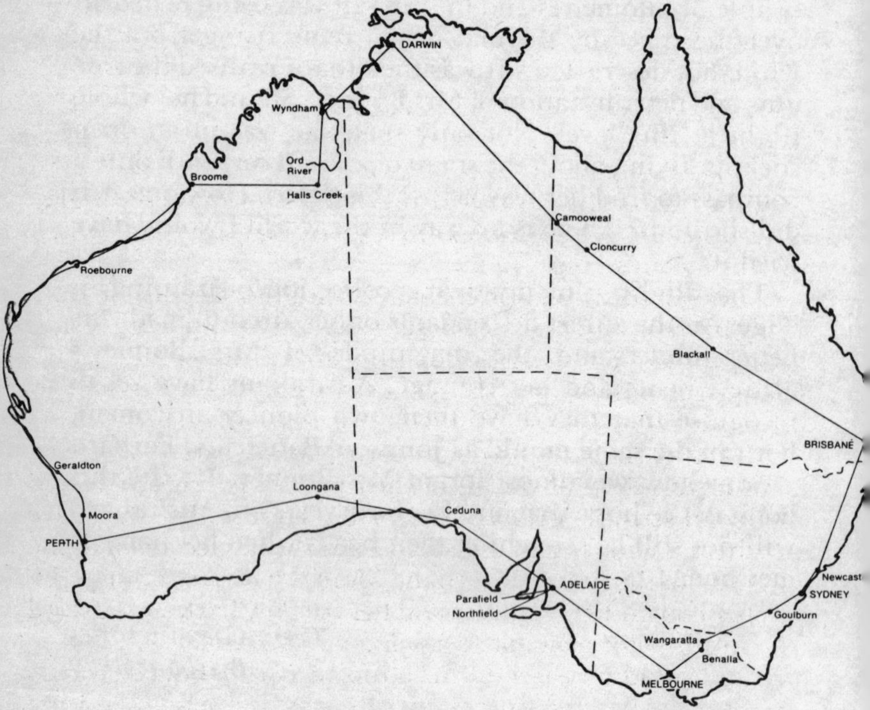

On 26 December 1931 Mrs Bonney set a new Australian record for distance covered in one day by flying 1524 km from Brisbane to Wangaratta. In 1932 she became the first woman to circumnavigate Australia by air, leaving Brisbane on 15 August and arriving back on 27 September.

Introduction

The tiny biplane was cruising 300 metres above the Malay coast and was almost within sight of Victoria Point, when the storm struck.

A hot bath, a good meal and a night's sleep were only minutes away. But for the dark-haired Australian woman at the controls her destination might just as well have been a million kilometres away. She was not going to make it.

Ugly black monsoonal storm clouds barred her way. The monsoonal storms of the tropics were rightly feared by all sensible pilots of the 1930s. To stay alive they gave them a wide berth. This had been the advice given to the pilot of the tiny de Havilland Moth, Mrs Lores Bonney, by her cousin Bert Hinkler and her friend Charles Kingsford Smith before she had set out from Brisbane.

She had seen the storms building earlier but she was so close to her landing point she was sure she could get through. Suddenly the black cloud above her opened up and she and her aircraft were engulfed in a torrential downpour. The rain seemed to fall in a solid mass. Visibility dropped to zero and she was unable to see even her instruments as the rain lashed her flying goggles. She tried to wipe the lenses clear but already her chamois leather flying gloves were sodden. She was forced to raise the goggles to see anything at all.

The rain stung her unprotected eyes and face like driving sand. The plane's small glass windscreen gave no protection to her open cockpit. The Moth bucked and rolled uncontrollably as it entered the furious centre of the storm. A sudden downdraught flung the aircraft into a rapid descent. The pilot desperately jammed the throttle fully open, urging every revolution possible from the Gipsy engine. But still the descent was unchecked. Unable to maintain height, the aircraft was heading for the white-crested waves, with the wind screaming through the rigging wires. She was 20 metres from a watery grave when the Moth escaped the grip of the storm and, with its propeller protesting, clawed its way slowly back up into the sky.

Temporarily clear of the cloud and rain, the terrified pilot for a moment wondered why on earth she had left her husband and home for such a mad adventure. However, quickly putting self pity aside, she took stock of the situation and planned her escape.

It was obvious that the storm was centred right over her destination and there was no way of getting through that day. It was already late afternoon and the storm would not die down till early next morning. She must turn back and find a suitable landing place on the coast. Airfields were rare in that part of the world in 1933, and she had neither the fuel nor sufficient daylight left to get back to Alor Star five hours to the south.

Then she remembered having flown over a small coastal island village half an hour earlier. At the time she had noted that a nearby strip of beach would have made an ideal emergency landing ground. It was her only chance. Threading her way between the pillars of rain now falling all around her, Mrs Bonney headed her aircraft, *My Little Ship*, back down the coast.

Thirty minutes later she arrived over the village. All seemed quiet. The only signs of life were several groups of buffalo grazing on a grassy patch at the edge of the beach. The tide was low and she could see a good area of flat hard water-packed sand clear of the surf. It was an ideal place to wait for the storms to clear.

She circled several times to pick the best landing spot and check the drift for the approach. She also made a note of the position of the buffalo. The last thing Mrs Bonney wanted was to hit one of the lumbering beasts on landing.

It would probably wreck her aircraft and secondly she had been warned that they were sacred animals on many of the islands, and she did not want to upset natives on whose assistance she might depend.

She set the Moth up on a long approach and throttled back into a gentle descent over the beach. The Dunlop balloon tyres kissed the wet flat sand on touchdown.

The tail was still up and she was keeping the landing roll straight with the rudder when she saw a buffalo lumbering right across her landing path. There was no time left to open the throttle and take off again, nor could she stop her aircraft in the short distance remaining. It had no brakes. There was only one thing left to do. She jammed on full rudder and swerved away from the unconcerned beast. At that point her luck ran out. The aircraft hit a spot where the beach dropped rapidly away and the surf broke onto the sand. A breaking wave caught the lower wing and slewed the aircraft straight into the incoming surf. There was a shower of spray and the Moth flipped over on its back in the sea.

As the biplane turned over and came to a sudden stop the pilot's head snapped forward against the padded cockpit coaming. She felt a sharp pain. Though dazed, she remained conscious. As she took in a sudden breath she choked as water poured down her throat. The cockpit was under water and she was in danger of drowning.

Mrs Bonney searched frantically for the pin to release her seat harness. She found it by feeling her way down the straps. But for some reason it would not release immediately. The pin was jammed. One thought flashed across her mind as she struggled to release the harness. What an inglorious finish to a record flight . . . drowning in her cockpit upside down!

Suddenly she was able to breathe again. The water had dropped away from her head. Though she was still pinned in the inverted aircraft, the cockpit was momentarily clear of water. She realised that she was only submerged when the waves came in. She took several long deep breaths before the next roller flooded over her.

After several minutes and a succession of waves she was

able to release the safety harness pin which had bent during the crash. She dropped head-first from the cockpit into shallow water and struggled up onto the beach. But for the still unconcerned buffalo it was deserted.

She flopped down on the beach and looked dejectedly at her wrecked plane. Only the wheels were totally visible above the surf. Between waves she could see its frail wood and fabric superstructure being pounded by the surf, and the tide was coming in.

'Oh my poor little ship,' she repeated over and over.

For the young woman, Lores Bonney, the dream to be the first airwoman to fly from Australia to England was shattered as surely as was her aircraft in the surf of Bang Biang Island off the coast of Malaya. The flight was over . . . the dream ended . . . or was it?

1
Taming the Rebel

Maude Rose (later 'Lores') Bonney was born in Pretoria, South Africa, on 20 November 1897. Her father, Norbert Albert Rubens, an importer, was of German and French descent. Her mother, Rose, was from Dutch and English stock.

The family moved to England when she was five years old and bought Ellerslie House, New Malden, in the London suburb of Wimbledon. They soon regretted the move. The dismal London winter with its chilling 'pea soup' fogs — a phenomenon well known in smoke-ridden London in the early twentieth century — was unbearable to a family raised in the heat of the South African sun.

After two years Norbert Rubens decided that they had had enough. Not wishing to return to a South Africa torn by the Boer War, he looked for a new homeland with warm sun and no wretched fogs. The family, he decided, would move to Australia.

Following a five-week voyage, the Rubens family arrived in Melbourne and settled in the suburb of Armadale. There Lores began her schooling. As she developed, two traits became obvious to her parents and teachers: her love of music and hate of discipline. She was a rebel. This rebellious side of her nature led to her being moved to several schools in an attempt to instil her with more discipline. For most of her junior and intermediate schooling she attended Cromarty Ladies College and the Star of the Sea Convent. At both schools her end of term reports consistently spoke of her artistic and musical ability, her dislike for scientific and mathematical subjects, and *always* of her independent nature.

As the daughter of a wealthy family in the Victorian era it was never considered that school should prepare Lores for any sort of career. In those days, it was more important that the daughters of wealthy families were well versed in the arts, sensible conversation and the social graces. The future role of refined young Victorian ladies was seen as the wife of a successful professional or businessman, capable of directing the servants, running the home and being the perfect hostess.

However, in 1911 Lores' Australian music professor suggested that his talented pupil should receive further training in Europe. Her parents decided that a finishing school in Europe might well be the solution. A couple of years of gently administered lady-like spit and polish would curb her rebellious nature and extend her musical ability.

Lores was enrolled at the Victoria Pensionat Finishing School in Germany.

Her new school was set in beautiful surroundings in Homburg, a suburb of Frankfurt. For the first few months she felt totally lost and out of her depth. Lessons were given in German and French and except for the one day of the week when she was able to converse in English, she sat miserably in class unable to understand a soul.

It was then that she first showed the tenacity which was to become a hallmark of her character in later years. She put her head down and studied the unfamiliar languages. In six months she had mastered them and was able to chatter fluently with her school mates. Suddenly she awoke to a new world of experience and was supremely happy.

With careful guidance her musical ability forged ahead and occasionally she had thoughts of becoming a concert pianist. At the school were young ladies from all over the world. Their descriptions of widely differing homelands and ways of life whetted the young Australian woman's appetite for travel. Already she was dreaming of seeing the world and absorbing its varied cultures. Too far from home to see her family during school holidays, she was allowed to travel around Europe accompanied by a teacher.

Among the less formal activities taught at the school was gardening. Each girl had her own small garden to tend. Lores found this a delightful hobby. Her love of flowers, fostered in Germany, was to have a profound effect on her later years.

It was there, too, that she gained her love for winter sports. When the first snows of the bitter German winter fell, the school's sunken tennis courts were flooded, providing a perfect skating rink. The girls also learned tobogganing on a nearby hill.

Slowly her rebelliousness began to disappear. Besides being happy within the school, she was enthralled by the every day pomp and circumstance that was a way of life for the privileged class in Kaiser Wilhelm's pre-war Germany. To a young girl, raised mainly in Melbourne, such things were understandably the most memorable moments of her stay in Europe. One of Lores' fondest memories was of the Kaiser himself. Quite often he would drive past the school, and he would always get his driver to blow the horn as he approached Victoria Pensionat. To the girls at the school this was a special occasion for they were allowed to leave their desks and wave *en masse* from their windows. Somehow the Kaiser heard of this special break in class discipline and always waved back to them.

The Kaiser's wife, the Kaiserin, also visited the school. Years later Lores Bonney still recalled one visit vividly.

'As she walked slowly along the line of girls she slowed down as she approached where I was standing. I was sure she was going to speak to me. But then she stopped at the girl next to me. I could have scratched the girl's eyes out I was so jealous. I studied the Kaiserin carefully and my eyes fixed on her jewellery. She was wearing row upon row of exquisite pearls. They immediately became my favourite jewel. Pearls have been an extravagance of mine ever since.'

Later that year she performed in front of the Kaiserin's sister, Princess Marguirita, who was the patroness of Victoria Pensionat. Following her piano recital she was introduced to the patroness and awarded the princess's special medal bearing the insignia of her regiment.

Shortly after her first concert appearance she was chosen to play at a public recital given by the school. As she took her place at the huge grand piano, she paused and glanced from the stage at the sea of faces all intent on her. Suddenly her nerves took control and she panicked. She could only think of one thing . . . getting off the stage. But how to do it without disgrace.

As a child in Australia she had been subjected to violent nose-bleeds when faced with situations and people she intensely disliked. 'There and then I decided that I neither liked the situation nor the sea of faces all looking straight at me,' she told me much later. 'I pretended to have a violent nose-bleed on the spot and fled from the stage!'

So ended Lores Bonney's first and last public concert appearance.

In 1914 her finishing period at Victoria Pensionat ended and she sailed home to Australia. During the six-week voyage the sixteen-year-old was fascinated by the people, places and new experiences at every port of call.

Among the passengers were a team of trapeze artists, the Pasquale Brothers. They were on their way to tour Australia. Like most showbusiness people they were outgoing and friendly and became popular with all the passengers. One of the aerialists in particular became the centre of the young Australian girl's attention.

'He was my first real crush. He was the handsomest man I ever met.'

A few weeks after she set sail, Arch Duke Ferdinand was assassinated at Sarajevo and Europe plunged into the Great War. Lores had left behind her the happiest two years of her childhood. When she stepped ashore in Melbourne her father saw a very different young lady to the gawky young rebel who had left them in 1911. Smartly dressed, well mannered, artistically educated, musically talented, she was a graceful young product of sophisticated Europe. And outwardly, at least, there were no signs of the rebel. However, behind the veneer of accepted conformity there still lurked a girl who was to challenge the traditional role of women long before women's liberation became a household word. No finishing school in the world was going to curb her inquisitive spirit and *wanderlust.*

As the nations of Europe descended into war, Australia soon became actively involved. The initial rush of young men volunteering to help the mother country soon became a flood. Women's involvement in this war was mainly out of uniform. But in steadily increasing numbers they joined the workforce filling the huge gaps left in the civilian ranks as the men joined up. Those women who did not take on a fulltime job joined the thousands of groups all over the country providing a wide range of aid and comforts to the men at the front. Welfare work kept Lores busy throughout the turbulent war years. Much of her time was spent working with Red Cross organisations.

Early in 1917 she met her future husband. While on a shopping expedition to the city she found herself short of money. She decided to go to her father's office and float a small loan. In her rush she ignored the secretary's protest that her father was busy. She knocked on the door and with typical youthful enthusiasm burst in to the office during the middle of a business meeting. Seated across the desk from Norbert Rubens was a tall, handsome man. Her father introduced him as Harry Bonney, a Brisbane leather goods manufacturer.

'We looked at each other and that was it. We were married later that year and I moved to Brisbane.'

Their first home in the Queensland capital was a suite of rooms in the downtown Gresham Hotel. The ornate and stately Gresham was a meeting place for the wealthy of Brisbane. It was also a favourite home away from home for graziers and their families when in town.

Only three years later the Gresham was to carve a niche in aviation history when Hudson Fysh, 'Ginty' McGinness, Fergus McMaster and others sat around one of the hotel's glass-topped tables and laid the foundations of Australia's great international airline, Qantas.

During their first few months of hotel luxury Lores

Bonney was busy settling down and exploring her new city. With a husband who spent long hours at Bonney and Clarke's leather goods factory, and no real home to entertain guests, Lores made few friends. After six months of hotel living she began to feel little more than a decoration. She had no real responsibilities and no home to organise.

Eventually she persuaded her husband that they should have a house of their own so that she could start taking on the responsibilities of a wife for which she had been so carefully and expensively trained. Too busy with his company commitments, he was glad to give her the job of finding them a suitable home.

Lores quickly found the ideal spot in Jordan Terrace on a steep rise of Bowen Hills. There they built a spacious Queensland-style home set on stumps which overlooked Breakfast Creek and the Hamilton Reach of the Brisbane River. As soon as they had moved in Lores set about organising the home and cultivating a beautiful garden. At last she felt she was using the talents so painstakingly gained at the Victoria Pensionat.

As Mrs Harry Bonney she moved easily into the social life of Brisbane's 'silvertails'. The war was over and with the coming of the mad roaring 'twenties business boomed and, like people the world over, Australians went on a dizzy happiness spree. To most women of that time Lores Bonney's lifestyle would have represented their dreams come true. A wealthy successful husband, beautiful home and a large circle of good friends. What more could a woman ask for?

But as the roaring 'twenties moved steadily towards the depressing 'thirties the tamed rebel within Lores Bonney began to loom into her consciousness. What had happened to that challenging, inquisitive spirit? Where was the woman who would see the world, experience its cultures and do something more than accept the traditional housewife role?

As the 'rebel' goaded her more and more she realised that despite her seemingly perfect situation, she had a real problem. She was bored stiff!

On 9 July 1926, as if to augur something of the future, a strange and inexplicable event took place in her life. She woke in the middle of the night from a vivid dream. In it she had seen an aircraft flying very close to the ground. She had quite clearly seen two men in the tandem open cockpits. Suddenly one of the crewmen slumped forward. The aeroplane had flown out of her sight with the stricken crewman hanging forward as though dead.

Next morning when she opened her daily newspaper she stared in confused disbelief at one of the headline stories.

English airman Captain Alan Cobham was flying from London in a de Havilland seaplane surveying the future airline route to Australia. He and his mechanic A. B. Elliott had made good progress until they ran into a massive dust storm on the Persian Gulf.

As they approached Basra the two men had been forced to descend to 20 metres to keep sight of the ground. They were picking their way over a huge area of swamp when there was an explosion in the front cockpit. Elliott slumped forward. Cobham throttled back the engine and shouted. 'Is there a fire?' Elliott managed to pass back a note to say that he had been hit by pieces of a broken petrol line and was losing lots of blood.

They raced for Basra. On arrival the mechanic was barely conscious and covered with blood. He was rushed to hospital but died that afternoon. When the wound was opened a bullet was found. An Arab had taken a potshot at the aircraft while they were flying low across the swamp!

The report concluded that Cobham was considering abandoning the flight. He and Elliott were close friends, in fact at the home airport, Stag Lane, they were known as the 'heavenly twins'.

Mrs Bonney was unable to find any explanation for her strange premonition.

2
A Bump for Location

In 1928 the most significant meeting in Lores Bonney's life took place. Her husband had invited friends to their home one weekend. Among the guests was a small, nuggety man who Harry Bonney introduced to his wife as his cousin. His name was Bert Hinkler.

In February of that year 'Hustling' Hinkler had made world headlines by completing the first solo flight from England to Australia. Following his triumphant arrival he had been lionised by the Australian public, but once all the ballyhoo died down and he attempted to find financial backers for a new aircraft he was planning to manufacture, the backslapping wellwishers and hangers-on rapidly vanished.

He had just completed a round-Australia tour in his record-setting Avro Avian biplane and was planning to return to England to set up a small aircraft-manufacturing company and produce his revolutionary Ibis amphibian. The project was eventually strangled by the Depression.

The young woman was fascinated by the airman. So used to conversations revolving around the same old parochial news and gossip, she listened spellbound to his discussion on aeroplanes. She noticed how the swarthy airman's grey eyes literally burned with enthusiasm when he talked of his plans and ambition to prove the safety of aircraft to a still doubting public. He profoundly believed that the answer to Australia's vast size and isolation from the rest of the world lay with the aeroplane.

When she casually mentioned that she had never been

up in an aircraft, Hinkler immediately suggested that he take her for a flight the next day. She jumped at the offer. Next morning, bundled up against the chilly winter westerly, she stood beside Hinkler's Avian at the Eagle Farm aerodrome. She watched intently as the airman carefully checked over the wire and fabric biplane. To her it looked incredibly graceful; a great silver bird perched awaiting flight.

Once all was ready, her cousin asked her if there was anywhere she particularly wanted to fly. Producing a huge bunch of roses she told him that she would like to deliver them to a dear friend in Yeerongpilly.

'Right, we'll deliver them by air.'

She climbed into the back seat with her huge bunch of home-grown roses and waited with almost uncontrollable excitement as the propeller was hand swung and the aircraft's Cirrus engine burst into life. Her famous pilot, noted for his perfectionist approach to flying and meticulous attention to detail, carefully performed a pre-flight check of the aircraft's instruments, control surfaces, and engine. Then with a sharp burst of power he turned the Avian into the wind.

Hinkler steadily opened the throttle, and keeping straight with a touch of the rudder, began the takeoff run across the tiny airport. Lores felt the seat boring into her back as the aircraft accelerated rapidly. The tail rose and a second later they were airborne. For Lores, the sensation was magnificent.

'It was the answer to my dreams. I had always adored birds for as long as I could remember. And there I was literally feeling like a bird.'

For the first few minutes she was speechless with excitement. She looked down with amazement at the Lilliputian world below. She quickly found her bearings and her voice and shouted directions for Hinkler to follow. She became acclimatised to finding her way from the new perspective, and had no trouble in identifying the house when they arrived overhead.

In the garden she saw her friend waving her arms 'like a windmill' as the aircraft circled the house. Hinkler reduced power and made a gentle swooping descent over the garden. At just the right moment Lores threw the flowers over the edge of the cockpit. To her great satisfaction they landed right alongside their human target. Not only had she shown that she was an able navigator, she had also displayed pinpoint accuracy as flower-bomb aimer.

When they landed back at Eagle Farm Hinkler complimented her on her navigation.

'He told me I had a pretty good "bump for location" — his phrase for good navigating. In later years I never forgot what he said and determined I would never get lost.'

She never flew with her cousin again. He returned to England and was tragically killed attempting a record flight to Australia in 1933.

But he had sown the seed of what was to become a lifelong passion. Life for Lores Bonney would never be quite the same again. She had flown.

* * *

Nearly two years passed before Mrs Bonney was to have the opportunity to learn to fly. She realised all along that her husband would not agree to her taking flying lessons. She was prepared to wait patiently for the right time.

Harry Bonney was a fanatical golfer. Every weekend he would spend his days at the Royal Queensland Golf Club. Lores was a golfing widow. At first she used to spend the hours alone in her garden but eventually her patience was exhausted. The boredom and loneliness was more than she could stand.

Her problem was magnified by the fact that although they owned two cars she could not drive. Her father had been violently opposed to women driving and Lores was sure Harry had come to a gentleman's agreement with her father when they married.

Eventually she decided that rather than spend her weekends alone at the house, she would go to the golf club with her husband. She had no intention of playing, but at least she could sit on the verandah with the other wives and talk over tea. And of course there was the added bonus of the aeroplanes. The Royal Queensland Golf Club was only a stone's throw away from Eagle Farm airport. All day aircraft buzzed overhead. She was reminded constantly of her trip with Bert Hinkler and the magnificent sensation of flight.

One Sunday as they drove through Hamilton for another long day at the golf club, she turned to her husband and asked to be let off at the airport. She had decided to sit at the aerodrome for the day and watch the aircraft for a change. He dropped her off at the airport which was little more than a cow paddock and arranged to meet her there later in the day.

'I had been standing watching for a while when a pilot of one of the Moths walked over to me. He asked me if I would like to go up for a joy flight. It would only cost ten shillings and he was sure I would enjoy it. I didn't give my husband's approval a second thought.'

On her second flight she again experienced the same exhilarating feeling of freedom she had eighteen months earlier with Bert Hinkler. She was 'hooked'.

During the next month she spent every weekend at Eagle Farm, and each time she took another passenger flight. Her pilot, she had discovered, was Charles Matheson. He ran a small flying school but when business was slow he augmented his income by giving joy rides. Occasionally he found a new student among his passengers. He soon sensed that Lores Bonney's interest was more than just a weekly joy ride, and one Sunday he suggested that he keep the dual controls in the passenger seat and let her try flying herself.

Though desperately keen to take the controls, she was still very worried about her husband's reaction if he knew she was taking lessons.

'I told him I would love to learn to fly but I did not think my husband would approve. When I told Captain Matheson that Harry would not even let me drive a car he just roared. "Do you mean to tell me that I am talking to a twentieth century wife who still does what her husband tells her. You really are unique." When he said that, I made my mind up right there and then. I would learn to fly but I would not let my husband know about it until I had gone solo.'

Charles Matheson was a fine instructor. Before they even went near the aircraft that morning he sat his new pupil down and quietly and patiently explained the rudiments of controlling an aircraft. He realised that at that early stage the young woman would not get the maximum benefit from an over-technical briefing. So he used her love and knowledge of birds to demonstrate the effect of the aircraft's controls.

'Imagine you are a bird. Now if you wanted to go to the left you would drop your left wing. If you wanted to soar up high you would lift your nose and if you wished to swoop down you would lower your nose, wouldn't you? Now take the control stick in your hand and use it the same way. Move it in the same direction as you want to go. Pretend your arms are your wings and use them as though you were a bird.'

So on the morning of 6 August 1930, in a de Havilland 60 Moth, registered VH-ULJ, Lores Bonney took her first flying lesson. It lasted exactly one hour.

'After that first flight with the stick in my hand I thought to myself, this is it. I finally knew there was only one real ambition in my life. I was going to learn to fly. I had found the control of the aircraft quite easy using my instructor's "bird technique". It gave me the sense of correct directional movement straight away. Taking off did not appear too difficult, the plane seemed to want to do it naturally if it had enough power. But I knew right from the beginning that the difficult part was getting down properly. That was going to be the hurdle.'

Her pilot log book tells the story of her clandestine early training. The entries increased as regularly as clockwork as she took one lesson a week, which was invariably at weekends. Occasionally she would squeeze in two flights while her unsuspecting husband was tramping the fairways late, trying to complete an extra nine holes.

As she progressed she became impatient. One day a

week was not enough. Somehow she had to find a way of getting to the aerodrome during the week. It was then that she used all her womanly cunning. For years she had made a habit of getting up very early and working in the garden. She would quite often be up with the first light at 5 a.m. while her husband slept in for several more hours. If she could find a way of getting to the aerodrome 5 kilometres away, she could sneak in a quick flight and be home before he was up and about.

Again the problem was the car. She cursed her lack of a driving licence. There must be someone about at that hour who could help, she thought. She was trying to solve the problem in her garden at dawn one morning when the solution came in person to the gate. It was the milkman on his early-morning rounds, stopping for a quick chat. She knew that his rounds took him out towards the aerodrome. She told him of her problem and within minutes he agreed to take her with him.

Captain Matheson, sworn to secrecy, also helped with her surreptitious dawn escapades. His mechanic passed close to her home and when the milkman was not available, he gave her a lift to and from the airport.

After three months she was impatient to go solo, but her instructor reminded her that she had to pass her aviation medical examination before he could send her up alone. She was more than ready. She had covered the required syllabus for solo flight, and had performed takeoffs, landings, turns, circuits, forced landings, stalls and spins all to Matheson's complete satisfaction.

Mrs Bonney kept putting off the visit to the aviation doctor for the check-up for fear he might let the cat out of the bag and inform her husband. Finally she realised she could procrastinate no longer.

However, when she left Dr McDonald's office later that day her world had collapsed. She was unable to make the medical standard required for a flying licence. During his examination he had found that she had a perforated eardrum. The government book of rules stated categorically that no one with this complaint could be issued with a pilot's licence.

For two weeks she moped around her house. Finally she decided to see if a specialist could help. She made an appointment to see Dr E. Couplin, the leading ear specialist. After an examination he told her that Dr McDonald's diagnosis was correct.

'But then he gave me some hope. He told me that though he could never do anything to bring back the hearing, he could scarify and close the perforation. The rule book said no perforated ear drum, and as far as he was concerned the perforation would be closed. The test for hearing? Well, that was another matter. In those days hearing was tested by the doctor whispering words to you across the room. Each ear was tested individually while you put your finger in the other. We had no trouble with my good ear, but when we came to the bad one, the dear man talked in an extremely loud whisper. After a period of treatment he signed a test form saying I had met the standard requirement. Dr McDonald was forced to accept me. For, besides being a specialist in private practice, Dr Couplin had also been appointed as ear specialist to the Air Board.'

Years after, Mrs Bonney liked to relate that incident to children planning some difficult undertaking. She believes strongly that if people decide to do something they should not let anything stand in their way.

'If you set your mind on something you can achieve it. There is no such word as "can't".'

While her treatment had been taking place Lores Bonney had continued her dual training. She knew the word had been secretly going around the aerodrome, among those who did not know of her medical problem, that Matheson would not send her solo because she was not good enough. 'Nobody needs that much dual training,' the mocking critics whispered.

On 22 November she proved them wrong, if only for five minutes! She took her Moth off from Eagle Farm, made one circuit of the aerodrome and landed safely on her own. Charles Matheson stood quietly on the ground watching his most determined pupil with a smile of satisfaction.

Her exhilaration on landing was tinged with apprehension. Now was the moment to break the news to her husband. She could not keep up the deception any longer; it was too nerve wracking. Her one hope was that now she had got this far, he would not disapprove. But no matter how much she loved flying she would not carry on with it without his approval. She cared too much for his feelings. She decided to phone him with her news. To her complete amazement he showered her with congratulations. He had known about her secret all along. She never discovered who had spilled the beans.

One year, almost to the day, after her first flight with Charles Matheson she gained her private licence. Testing officer Wyn Pike commented after the forty-five minute examination flight, that her performance was as good as any he had ever seen.

Her husband, who openly encouraged her once the 'secret' was out, was delighted with the news. So much so that when a suggestion of her own aircraft was casually made, he immediately told her to look for a suitable machine.

She was soon the proud owner of a DH 60. Officially it was registered VH-UPV, but to Lores Bonney it was the name she painted on the cowling, *My Little Ship*. For the next two months she trained in blind flying, and cross country navigation. She also took a friend for a flight. It was her first passenger-carrying trip. But already she was getting itchy feet. She had an aeroplane and a licence. It was time to start seeing some of that world.

With the support and encouragement she needed from Harry Bonney she decided to make a long distance cross country flight. The one other person she wanted to share her new experience with was her father. He had moved from Melbourne and had bought a home at Wangaratta, Victoria, 1600 kilometres away. She decided to fly down to see him and keep an earlier promise she had made to join the family for a special dinner on Boxing Day. It would be her first solo cross country flight. But there was one problem to solve. Traditionally she and her husband had always eaten Christmas Dinner at Lennons Hotel. It was a special occasion and she would not dream of disappointing him by leaving Brisbane before Christmas. There was only one possible solution. She would fly down to her father's home in one day.

In a world accustomed to today's jet travel that might seem a minor hurdle. However, Mrs Bonney's Moth only cruised at 125 km/h. To get there before dark she would have to leave at dawn.

She took off with the first signs of day at 4.30 a.m. climbing steadily away from Archerfield Aerodrome into the daylight. Three hours later she had refuelled at Coffs Harbour and set out for Sydney's Mascot Aerodrome. The flight was uneventful until she crossed Broken Bay. She was alarmed to see that the air bubble in the glass tube that indicated the level of her fuel tank disappeared. Either it was faulty or she was nearly out of fuel.

In an interview with the Brisbane *Courier* Mrs Bonney said:

'Seeing a yacht moving in the same direction I decided to fly over the water and land on it [the water] if necessary, with the chance of being picked up by the people in the yacht, rather than risk a forced landing amongst the trees and cliffs on the land. I also flew to a higher altitude so that, if I must come down, I should have a greater gliding distance. Again, when I was going over the thickly settled suburbs of Sydney the thought of a forced landing was disconcerting. However, I reached Mascot aerodrome safely.'

Once on ground a mechanic inspected her fuel system. There was still fifteen minutes fuel left in the tanks. The problem, he assured her, was a faulty fuel gauge. While she was waiting at Mascot, flying instructor Captain Follet tried to persuade the airwoman not to continue with the flight. Her landing had not been a good one, due probably to her concern over her fuel situation, and he was convinced the long flight was too much for a woman. Mrs Bonney was not impressed!

Thirty minutes later she was on her way again. She arrived at Cootamundra at 4.30 in the afternoon after stopping to refuel at Goulburn. She was running later than planned due to strong head winds across New South Wales.

While checking her engine prior to takeoff from Cootamundra the throttle jammed and she was delayed even further while it was repaired. It was nearly 5.15 p.m. when she finally took off on the last leg of her flight. Strong winds and the late afternoon heat made flying conditions difficult and *My Little Ship* was constantly thrown around by the turbulence.

The setting sun and smoke haze reduced her forward visibility to such an extent that she was eventually forced to descend to 300 metres in order to navigate. Throughout the flight she had held course by the use of maps and compass, but as the visibility worsened she was forced to keep track of her position by every available means. Twice she resorted to circling low over towns and reading the names on the railway stations. Thus she was able to pin point Wodonga and Chiltern. As she approached her destination she flew low over a country homestead. Within seconds half a dozen people rushed out into the yard and all pointed in one direction. The word had obviously spread that she was coming.

Last light was approaching as she came in sight of the landing ground at Wangaratta. A crowd of people were there to welcome her. The first person to rush out to meet her, as she taxied in through the long grass, was her father. He was so overcome with excitement that he failed to realise the engine was still ticking over. Mrs Bonney froze with fear when she saw him running towards the still rotating propeller. She swerved to save him from certain death.

A reporter from the *Age* who was at the aerodrome wrote:

'As Mrs Bonney's silver and blue Gipsy Moth plane settled gracefully after circling the field, a slim girl in a leather helmet and very feminine looking crash overall stepped out of the cockpit with the utmost self possession and modest assurance, as if flying from Brisbane were an every day occurrence for her. "We had a wonderful trip and nothing exciting happened," she told a representative of the *Age*. When complimented on her fresh and vigorous appearance she remarked, "I feel splendid! Take to the air if you want to be fit." And, indeed, her looks justified the advice. Mrs Bonney is a most attractive girl, very petite and with dark curly hair.'

It is probable that the reporter from the *Age* did not look too closely beyond the pretty face. Had he done so he would have seen that she was in fact exhausted. It was sixteen hours since she had left Archerfield and she had been airborne for fourteen-and-a-half hours of that time.

That evening, as promised, she sat down to the special family dinner with her parents and friends. Their happiness was enhanced by the news that Mrs Bonney had set a record with her flight. Until that time the longest single flight by an Australian airwoman had been less than 600 kilometres. In a single day she had beaten that figure by a staggering 1000 kilometres!

For Lores Bonney the importance of the flight was not the record, but rather that she had proved to herself her ability to navigate long distances over unknown country. Moreover, she was now confident that she was physically capable of combating the rigours of long distance flying. And, unknown to the happy band of family and friends who gaily chattered around the dinner table that night, the airwoman already had a more challenging flight in mind.

3
Around Australia

Mrs Bonney's next goal was to circumnavigate Australia by air. True, it had been done before: S. J. Goble and Ivor McIntyre had shown the way in 1924 flying a Fairey IIID seaplane. It had taken them forty-five exhausting days. Captain E. J. Jones of the Civil Aviation Department then improved the record by doing it in twenty-two-and-a-half days. In 1927 Charles Kingsford Smith and Charles Ulm did it in a bid to get publicity and raise finance for their planned trans-Pacific flight. They had slashed the record to ten days and five hours. Since then a few other men had made the flight.

But by 1932 no airwoman had yet taken on the challenge. Most airmen considered the flight over thousands of kilometres of inhospitable and unpopulated outback unsuitable for a woman. Harry Bonney was no exception.

'Knowing my husband as I did, I was aware that if I went to him and said that I wanted to fly around Australia it would be thumbs down. However, his mother was living in Western Australia at the time. So one day I said to him . . . "Wouldn't it be lovely to fly over and see her"? He thought it was a great idea. I let him digest that for a while, then suggested to him that rather than go all that way straight there and back, it would be much more interesting to go up around the top and back around the bottom. So that was how I got him to agree without his fully realising what I was taking on!'

In the weeks following her return from Wangaratta Mrs Bonney had been studying hard for her 'B' (commercial) licence. The ground examinations had been her major worry. Her dislike for mathematical subjects had not changed since her school days, but realising that a good knowledge of these subjects was imperative if she was to pass, she had been studying day and night. For her navigation theory she had enlisted the aid of Captain Wall, a retired sea captain, and with his tutoring she had grasped the intricacies of course, track, drift, deviation and variation.

When she sat her theory examinations in February 1932 she passed them all on her first attempt.

Meanwhile, she had continued her flying training with Cyril Broome at the Royal Queensland Aero Club. She had progressed well with her advanced sequences and had eventually been tested.

'The examiner that day gave me quite a fright. Before we had even started the test he told me that I didn't have much hope of passing. I have never been able to figure out whether he was trying to unnerve me and see if I could still cope with the test, which was reasonable to expect of a commercial pilot, or whether he just didn't think that any woman could possibly fly well enough to be a commercial pilot. Flying was almost exclusively a man's domain, particularly when it came to commercial aviation. Anyway when the test was over he congratulated me on my performance and told me I had passed the manipulative test flight with flying colours.'

The wheels of bureaucratic red tape turned as slowly in 1932 as they often do today. When she departed from Archerfield Aerodrome on 15 August 1932 to fly around Australia she had still not received official advice that she had been granted her commercial licence. Not that it really mattered for she had no intention of carrying any passengers, let alone those who might wish to buy a ticket. Like her famous cousin Bert Hinkler, Lores Bonney preferred to make her long distance flights alone.

Her planned route via Darwin, Port Hedland, Perth, Kalgoorlie, Adelaide, Melbourne, Sydney and back to Brisbane was close to 13000 kilometres. It would be considered quite an undertaking by a new commercial pilot in today's fast reliable light aircraft. But for a pilot with only 221 hours total flying time, in an aircraft which was slower than most modern cars, it required a great faith in her own and her aircraft's reliability to even contemplate such a long, lonely flight.

But for Mrs Bonney such faith was a matter of course. On all her flights she never considered she was doing it totally solo. Her deep religious belief made her quite sure that she always had the best co-pilot in the world alongside.

'It never struck me that I would not make it on any of my long flights. I wasn't worried one scrap. I had faith in God, in myself and in my aeroplane. What more did I need?'

The first leg of the flight was to the central Queensland mining town of Blackall. A crowd of wellwishers had gathered at Archerfield to see her off.

When asked by a Brisbane *Daily Mail* reporter what he thought of the airwoman's chances of completing the flight, Wyn Pike, an examiner for the Civil Aviation Department, replied,

'She will be all right. There is no reason why she should not succeed. She will do well to confine her flying to five hours a day, however, so as not to risk landing in bad light, and to relieve the strain which must occur on a flight of this nature.'

One of her Aero Club instructors, Frank Gardiner, was not so confident. 'It is rather a big effort for a woman,' he said. Time and time again Mrs Bonney had come up against this attitude that because she was of the 'weaker sex', her chances weren't good. This despite her proven flying ability. Even when she had discussed the flight with Charles Kingsford Smith and asked him what he felt her chances were, he had answered, 'You might make it if you've got the guts.'

Such comments often incensed her, but they did have a beneficial spin off as they made her more determined than ever to do her thing.

The last person to farewell the airwoman as she strapped into the tiny cockpit was her husband. It had long before become obvious to him that the flight was something more than just a visit to see his mother. But he had made no effort to discourage his wife. He had already realised that she had found a love in her life with which he could not compete. An intelligent, generous and loving husband, he gave her total support and encouragement — both financially and emotionally.

It took Lores Bonney eight hours to reach Blackall; three more than the daily limit recommended by examiner Wyn Pike. The following morning the Brisbane *Daily Mail* explained why:

'Blackall, Monday — Mrs Bonney landed at Blackall Aerodrome at 5.45 p.m. After passing over Tambo and following a telegraph line for about twenty minutes, Mrs Bonney concluded she was off course. She turned back and corrected her error.

'A few minutes later she noticed that petrol was flowing freely from the carburettor. Considering it inadvisable to continue, Mrs Bonney landed at Macfarlane Downs, half way between Tambo and Blackall.

'Mr Doyle, the owner of the station, helped her to rectify the trouble and after a considerable delay the flight was resumed.'

In fact, while she was taking off from Macfarlane Downs, the throttle problem that had delayed her on the Wangaratta flight recurred. However, her time spent with Qantas engineer Arthur Baird, learning to service her aircraft in preparation for the flight, paid off. A sharp knock released the jammed linkage.

She arrived at Blackall at 5.45 p.m., grabbed a steaming cup of tea, and immediately began to work on the aircraft in preparation for the next day.

Low winter temperatures had contributed to the day of aggravating mechanical problems. Her husband had anticipated the cold, and had made her suede overalls, leather leggings, and a leather overcoat for the trip. But despite these precautions she had almost frozen to death in the cockpit.

The next morning, after adding an extra layer of clothing beneath her Bonney and Clarke leather flying gear, she climbed aboard her Moth and was airborne by 8.30 a.m. After refuelling at Longreach she was assisted by a tail wind and made good time, reaching Cloncurry for mid-afternoon tea. Her only problem had been a period of severe turbulence which had bumped her about in the cockpit bruising both her arms.

While there she met Qantas pilot Lester Brain, who was doing the outback mail run from Cloncurry to Camooweal, the route she was to follow that day. When he suggested that she tag along for the company, she accepted immediately. It seemed good sense to have the added safety precaution of another aircraft over the desolate stretch of country.

Camooweal was in a festive mood the afternoon the two aircraft arrived. The annual picnic races were being held the next day and the town was packed with people from kilometres around. The townspeople begged her to stay over for the races. Though sorely tempted, she had to keep to her schedule; her next hop was 1200 kilometres to Darwin. She did, however, agree to judge the children's fancy dress competition at the race ball that night. She was in bed early.

'They said I couldn't do it in a day, but I've done it!' Mrs Bonney told reporters when she landed at Darwin at 5.15 p.m. on the fourth day of her flight.

Following a delay of one-and-a-half hours getting the engine started at Camooweal that morning, she had set out for Daly Waters at 7 a.m. She landed at noon and was delayed again for over an hour with spark plug trouble. She found the navigation north to Darwin relatively simple. As planned, she followed the rough motor track. She had no trouble identifying it. The route was littered with empty fuel cans tossed away by motorists!

The only very uncomfortable moment was in the Mataranka area where bush fires choked the sky with dense smoke. Unable to fly over or around the black cloud, she had been forced to go through it and had found it almost suffocating.

She made a rather bumpy landing at Darwin. 'I was not accustomed to the lighter and more humid air,' she told pressmen, tongue in cheek. Mrs Bonney had completed one-quarter of her trip around the continent. Her actual flying time, so far, stood at twenty-three hours and ten minutes. The 1200 kilometres to Darwin that day had been covered in eight hours actual flying time.

At Darwin the airwoman had a day free from the rigours of outback flying. Her engine was due for a Top End overhaul and while this was looked after by the airport engineers, she took time out to explore Australia's northern frontier town.

Her hosts at the Hotel Victoria paid her a great tribute by putting her in the Aviators' Room. The only airmen allowed to stay in this room were the record breakers. Former occupants had included Kingsford Smith, Hinkler, Scott and Mollison, all on their record-breaking England-Australia flights.

On the afternoon of her day off she couldn't keep away any longer! She hurried out to the airport and in greasy overalls spent the next three hours assisting engineer Cowper. Her final job that afternoon was to clean up a large quantity of chocolate which had melted in the front cockpit where she stored survival rations for the flight.

That night she went to bed early in anticipation of the next day's flying. Coming up was the leg she dreaded. Darwin-Wyndham-Ord River. Her maps showed a rugged, desolate, and virtually uninhabited land.

A journalist in Darwin recorded her departure next morning in a somewhat patronising style,

'The sun was rising as the machine rose, and the light made the aeroplane glitter like a golden dragonfly. She circled several times, rising to a good altitude, then flew in the direction of Wyndham. "She is the prettiest woman flyer we have ever seen," say the local girls. "And businesslike and practical," add the mechanics.'

She set off for Wyndham at 7 a.m. and arrived three hours later. In a telegraphed message to the Brisbane *Sunday Mail* she said,

'I had a dreadful trip over Queens Channel. It was very, very difficult, and the way was not certain at Cape Domett, as I was relying on flying a compass course.

'I was never so glad to see a place in my life as I was to see Wyndham. I picked out the aerodrome after a time and landed, after circling for about half an hour, on a salt marsh. The machine is still whole.

'On the way fog and cloud caused bad visibility and made low flying necessary. This made it hard to follow my map for any great distance.'

At midday she was off again heading for Ord River Station. She experienced difficulties with her aircraft compass on this leg of her flight. In fact for a while she was quite lost.

She had been told that she might encounter severe inaccuracies in her compass over this area before making the flight.

'I had been warned that the huge deposits of ironstone (ore) in the mountains of the North-West would probably affect my compass and make it difficult to fly a true course. Surveyors, I was told, had experienced difficulty as a result of this magnetic interference. I determined to take extra precautions to minimise the danger of getting lost, however these precautions were of little use. There were virtually no identifiable features on the ground to read off my map. Holding what I hoped was an accurate compass course I flew on and on, trying to find some prominent landmark I could identify. It was hopeless. I was completely lost over some of the most inhospitable country in the world. There was nowhere I could have landed and if the worst had happened I would have undoubtedly written off my machine and probably myself.'

She climbed to 1800 metres and backtracked along her course, mentally preparing herself for a crash landing in the bush. She was particularly worried about being the subject of a massive search similar to one mounted only four months earlier for two lost German airmen, Hans Bertram and Adolf Klausmann. They had been found by an Aboriginal, forty-four days after a forced landing 90 kilometres from Wyndham, just when they had (in their own words) 'laid down to die'.

She had given up all hope of completing the flight. 'I

was bitterly disappointed. "This is where you use your tucker bag," I told myself, "Australia has you beaten." I then determined to make one more attempt to locate a station and headed in a new direction across an area of unbroken timber.'

Ten minutes later she spotted a small group of buildings. On landing she found she was well off course and had dropped in on Flora Valley Station. There she was met by two local 'cockies' complete with grass stalks hanging from their mouths. Looking her up and down the taller one turned to his dusty companion and drawled, 'Yer know mate, can't be much in this flying business after all, if a woman can do it.' Mrs Bonney turned and gave him a pitying smile. However, after a cup of tea and a new set of directions, she was on her way again. Late that afternoon she arrived at Ord River Station.

En route from Ord River to Halls Creek the next day, she again encountered navigational problems with her compass, and surprised the owner of Flora Valley Station when she visited him for the second day running. She eventually reached Halls Creek after lunch. The nightmare stretch was over, but even at the very last moment things went wrong. On arrival she made a very heavy landing and damaged the Moth's undercarriage. The starboard leg collapsed and the aircraft slewed to a stop on its wing tip.

Lores Bonney was already beginning to gain a reputation for a landing technique that was eventually to earn her the nickname of the 'rock wallaby' in aviation circles.

'I often made several bounces before my aircraft finally settled onto the ground!' she told me much later.

'Aircraft of that era were not designed for easy landing as are today's light aircraft. They had no landing flaps and employed two main wheels and a wood and metal tail skid. Unless the pilot touched down in a perfect "three point" attitude, at the correct speed, the aircraft would bounce.'

With her undercarriage temporarily repaired Mrs Bonney set out for Broome next day. Five-and-a-half hours later she was searching the horizon ahead when she saw it. For a moment or two she saw a dark line on the bush horizon. Within minutes the line had turned to a glittering blue ribbon — the Indian Ocean — she had flown coast to coast! After circling the tiny town she made a perfect landing at 1.30 p.m.

As a memento of her crossing, the residents of the pearling town presented her with a beautifully carved set of her initials in their local mother of pearl. Broome reminded her of the love for pearls she had acquired at the Victoria Pensionat nearly twenty years before.

Her flight down the west coast to Perth took three days. She had overnight stops at Roebourne, Geraldton and Moora. She had no problems with navigation, she merely followed the coast. However, as she flew further south the weather suddenly deteriorated. She made an abortive attempt to leave Geraldton and was forced back by heavy rain. Twenty-four hours later she got through as far as Moora, where she was forced to land in a paddock 12 kilometres from town.

From Moora to Perth she hit a seemingly endless series of rain squalls. The wind and precipitation were the worst she had ever encountered. Violent turbulence threw her aircraft all over the place. During one particularly jarring patch of turbulence she heard a definite cracking sound. From there on she was aware of an intermittent vibration. But at that stage she had her hands too full to worry about it.

'The rain was pouring down, visibility was reduced to a few hundred yards, and for most of the journey I had been forced down to tree top height. To add to my discomfort it was extremely cold. More than once I was tempted to turn back. I was never more thankful than when I saw Perth ahead.'

As she flew over the city she was met by an escort of four Moths from the West Australian Aero Club. They formed up behind her aircraft as she approached Maylands Aerodrome. However, her plane was much faster than the club aircraft and they had great difficulty in keeping up.

Her mother-in-law, representatives of the Aero Club

and a group of Royal Australian Air Force pilots on an aerial survey mission, watched as she landed. She had reached the halfway point.

The next day as mechanics were going over her aircraft they discovered a broken spar in her lower starboard wing. The mystery of the snapping noise and unexplained vibration was solved. It is probable that the damage was caused when the undercarriage had collapsed at Halls Creek. The turbulence coming into Perth had merely finished the job. The Aero Club's chief flying instructor, Max Allen, stated she was lucky to have made Perth without serious mishap.

A week passed before her aircraft was ready to continue the flight. A new spar was fitted and the engine overhauled. On 4 September she set off on the long flight home.

She had intended to fly as far as Forrest on the first day. She reached the gold mining town of Kalgoorlie by lunch time and after quickly refuelling she was on her way again. However, head winds slowed her down and as darkness approached she was still 100 kilometres short of her destination.

Mrs Bonney's luck held out. She sighted a tiny town below and decided to land. In failing light she picked a landing area.

'How I managed to get down in one piece at Loongana on Sunday night I don't know,' she reported by telegraph to the *Daily Mail*. 'Luck was with me, as in failing light I put the aircraft down on a shockingly rough rocky surface. Any moment I expected the tail skid to be wrenched off but my luck held — and also the skid.'

Everyone in the tiny town came out to meet her. On their advice she moved the aircraft to another area. Once on the ground it was obvious that there would be insufficient space for a fully loaded takeoff next day. She lightened her aircraft by removing luggage and rations, and with the aid of a lantern took off in the dark and flew a few hundred metres to a better takeoff area.

The next day she crossed the great Nullarbor Plains and arrived in Ceduna. On 7 September she landed at

Adelaide's Parafield Aerodrome. There she reported a strange 'tinkling' noise in her Gipsy motor but following an engine 'run-up' the Parafield ground crew were unable to find any problem.

Journalists at the airport were the first to hear a startling piece of news as they interviewed Mrs Bonney. It was dropped in quite casually amid a discussion on her life. The report was published next day.

'There are two Mrs Bonneys. One spent this morning tinkering with the engine of her Gipsy Moth she is flying around Australia. The other went to the Violet Farm this afternoon.

'One Mrs Bonney wants to fly to England . . . "I am strong enough and capable enough and I have taken a course in navigation with Captain Wall, and when I return to Brisbane I shall take up night- and blind-flying seriously."

'"But is it fair to my husband?" asks Mrs Bonney Number Two. "A long flight is a heavy strain on those who are left behind; besides I am a married woman, and have a responsibility to my home."'

It was obvious during her interview with the press that Lores Bonney the rebel and Mrs Harry Bonney the conventional housewife were engaging in a preliminary skirmish for a battle royal yet to come. Deep down she probably knew already who would win. It is almost certain that on reading the report, her husband would have guessed the outcome and was already mentally preparing for another period as a grass widower!

Later in the article it became obvious that she decided she had better attempt to make it appear that the final decision would not be hers. Like any 'properly brought up woman' she would leave the decision to her husband.

'"I know 'hubs' will forbid me if I ask his permission, and I must not disobey him,"' she added.

How to make a flight to England, without asking Harry Bonney's permission, was a problem that would exercise her mental gymnastics throughout the remainder of the flight. Still she had managed to learn to fly without his permission, and she had also managed to set off on a round-Australia flight, after a little cunning planning, with hubs' blessing. No doubt she would find a way. But first she had to finish this trip and she still had a long way to go.

She almost didn't make it. Ten minutes after taking off from Parafield, on 8 September, her Gipsy engine started to backfire. The power fell off rapidly and she started to lose height. Desperately she searched for a forced landing field. She was in luck. Just ahead she sighted a clear paddock and landed safely near the Northfield Hospital.

When *My Little Ship* arrived by road at Parafield later that day engineers stripped down the engine. The trouble wasn't hard to find. There was a hole the size of a ten cent piece in one of the pistons. Mrs Bonney's luck had held again. Had it happened ten minutes later she would have been over the rough, wooded Adelaide foothills with nowhere suitable to land.

The next day's newspaper carried a brief account of the mishap, and also a comment that she had denied earlier reports that she wanted to fly to England. She had never given the flight any consideration and certainly would not attempt it in a single-engined aeroplane! It seems that Mrs Bonney had decided that she had better get everybody's mind off that flight for now, particularly her husband's. She should wait for a more opportune moment to broach that subject again.

Five days later she was off again. With her engine overhauled she made Melbourne in seven-and-a-half hours. She was two hours late in arriving and confessed on landing that she had reached Melbourne on time but had found difficulty in locating Essendon Aerodrome and had been circling the outskirts of the city. 'Just like a woman,' someone in the crowd unkindly remarked. Mrs Bonney either did not hear or chose to ignore the male chauvinist opinion.

From Melbourne she flew on to Wangaratta, accompanied by the Shell Company aircraft. Shell had done her fuelling throughout the flight.

A large crowd headed by her father was waiting at the airport. On landing she was officially greeted by the shire chairman and to her surprise she was led over to a brand new aircraft hangar. On the tiny building was painted 'The Bonney Hangar'. It had been built especially to house her aircraft. The local people had raised the £42 10s 6d required for the building materials and volunteers had erected it in two days!

Shortly after, she told her father some exciting news that she had heard from the Civil Aviation Department in Melbourne. She had been officially awarded her commercial pilot's licence.

Three days later the newspaper headlines read 'Collision at 2000 ft' . . . 'Mrs Bonney's Escape' . . . 'Wing Ripped'.

After leaving Wangaratta bound for Benalla, *My Little Ship* had again been accompanied by the Shell Company aircraft. On board were company pilot Harold Owen and a photographer, J. T. Harrison. They had decided to get some photographs of Mrs Bonney and her plane from the air. They had taken several from the one position and were re-positioning for a close-up when the two aircraft collided.

'It was the narrowest escape I've known,' Mrs Bonney told reporters afterwards. 'Had I not been following my usual practice of flying as high as 2000 feet whenever possible, nothing would have saved us from a terrible crash.

'I left Wangaratta at about 10 a.m. this morning to fly over to Benalla to attend a public luncheon in my honour. Mr Owen and Mr Harrison decided to accompany me to take photographs.

'When we were near Glenrowan Mr Harrison wanted to take a close-up and Mr Owen manoeuvred his machine close under mine on the left side. Suddenly an air current caught us, either forcing my aircraft down or Mr Owen's upward, I could not tell which.

'To my horror the tail of his aircraft collided with my wing and we remained locked together for about two seconds. Then the left wing of the other aircraft tilted vertically and dropped like a stone.'

Pilot Owen had a real problem with a severely mangled

tailplane. His instinctive and correct action when the aircraft locked together was to pull away and drop down to the left to prevent any further damage. This he did, only to find the aircraft almost uncontrollable without a working rudder. They spun down while he struggled to regain control. They were within 70 metres of the ground when he corrected the dive and was able to control his Moth to a heavy but safe landing in open country.

Mrs Bonney's aircraft was less seriously damaged and she was able to land safely at Benalla, once she had seen the two men safely out of their downed aircraft. *My Little Ship* had a large tear in the wing fabric and some broken wing ribs. It was quickly repaired and she flew back to Wangaratta later in the day.

The flight back to Brisbane via Sydney and Newcastle took three days. She had hoped to fly non-stop from Sydney but was forced to turn back and land at Newcastle after hitting severe rain storms over the ranges. They extended well out to sea so there was no hope of getting through. She spent an extra frustrating day in Newcastle when it was discovered the next morning that the rain-soaked grass aerodrome was like a bog and aircraft could not take off.

On 27 September the cyclone that had brought the bad weather passed out to sea, and the weather along Mrs Bonney's route was slowly improving. Determined to get home that day she battled against strong winds and low cloud up the coast to Brisbane. From Southport on, the weather worsened and she was forced down to 150 metres to get through.

At 1.20 p.m. she landed at Archerfield Aerodrome. As she taxied in, the wind had one final go at her. A sudden gust tipped her Moth onto one wing but again 'Bonney's Luck' was with her. The aircraft righted itself and was undamaged. When she finally put the mixture into full lean, closed the ignition switched and felt the propeller judder to a halt she had covered the 12 800 kilometres in ninety-five hours' flying time and had been away forty-three days.

It was not the fastest time by any means, but to Mrs

Bonney that did not matter. She had never tried to be the fastest. It was more important for her to be the first among the small but growing band of world airwomen to fly around Australia. Even more importantly she saw it as a 'warm-up' for the much longer and more difficult flight to England, that by now she was determined to do. But first she must get Harry Bonney's permission, without giving him a chance to forbid the flight. That was going to take some doing.

4
England Bound

Mrs Bonney decided that the only way to win her husband's approval for a flight to England was to be so completely prepared before she even raised the subject that he could not find the smallest technical reason for her *not* to make the flight.

She studied every possible aspect of the flight in detail. Her round-Australia trip had proved her ability to navigate long distances over harsh featureless wilderness. It had also ensured she could not be challenged on her ability to withstand the physical and mental rigours associated with long-distance flying.

She had flown in foul weather conditions that in her opinion were as bad as any she might encounter on her way to England. She had successfully handled engine failure in flight, undercarriage failure on landing, structural failure of a wing spar and a mid-air collision. Her actual flying ability was beyond question. She was one of the world's select little band of women commercial pilots. What else did she need to prove her total self-sufficiency for the England flight?

One problem has been apparent on her previous flights. Having only a limited mechanical knowledge she had been very much dependent on the assistance of ground engineers for servicing and repairs to her Moth and its Gipsy engine. Around Australia such assistance was never too far away. But on a flight to England it would be a different matter indeed. Across South-East Asia, India and the Middle East established aerodromes were few and far between. Admittedly outposts of the

Royal Air Force were flung across the Empire. But they were thousands of kilometres apart. At most of her planned landing grounds it would be difficult enough to find a refueller, let alone anyone with a mechanical knowledge of her aircraft.

She would have to undertake her own routine servicing and also be able to supervise untrained people should any major mechanical repairs be required. To do this she would need a complete understanding of the servicing and overhauling techniques of *My Little Ship*, particularly its 100 hp four-cylinder Gipsy engine.

By today's standard the engine was not as complicated as the car motor. But for nearly 20000 km her life would depend on its reliability and that would require constant and scrupulous attention. If it stopped she couldn't just pull over to the side of the road.

She approached Arthur Baird, chief engineer of Qantas, the airline which serviced and maintained her aircraft. The engine was due for a major overhaul and Mrs Bonney suggested that she do the work under supervision. Baird was quite amazed with her enthusiasm and total involvement with flying. Naturally he did not know the reason behind her request. He agreed to let her work in his maintenance shop as an unofficial apprentice.

Mrs Bonney was fortunate to employ a most efficient housekeeper who kept the home front running smoothly while her employer covered herself with overalls and grease at Archerfield.

Still unable to drive a car, she caught the tram to the terminus on Ipswich Road, then walked or hitched a lift the last couple of kilometres through farming country to Archerfield. She always arrived at 8 a.m. sharp each morning and waited with a small group of men for the workshop to open. Five minutes later she was at her work bench. She took an hour for lunch and then continued work till 5 p.m.

Mrs Bonney's arrival on the scene was quite a shock to the staff of the maintenance hangar. It was a man's world. Initially some viewed her intrusion into their domain in much the same way as if she had entered the bar of their favourite watering hole. But she was there with the boss's blessing so they kept their thoughts to themselves.

However, she was subjected to some unmerciful teasing in the beginning. Some of the older hands were unable to take her seriously. George Ditchman, who now runs his own aircraft maintenance business, was a young Qantas apprentice at the time.

'I remember very clearly when Mrs Bonney was working in our shop. Some of the men thought it was all a big joke. She was the subject of many practical jokes. Often we would drop a small part from her engine, or a tool, into one of the big oil baths and ask her to fish it out. She never backed down at anything and would plunge her arm, up to the shoulder, into the big vat of dirty black oil. She really surprised us because she was a good looking young woman and a silvertail too, yet she took it all with a smile. She really was a good sport and soon earned everyone's respect.'

They were amused by her habit of writing page after page of notes in a little book during every stage of the overhaul. One day a mechanic got his hands on her notebook and read it through. He and his mates had very red faces when they found pertinent personal comments she had entered about them and the jokes they had played on her. She had been wise to them all along.

The days she did not enjoy were when they had to remove the thick black deposits of carbon from the engine. The parts had to be boiled in a special solution to be cleaned.

'Mr Davies, my engineering instructor, took a personal delight in informing me when the parts needed cleaning in the boiling phenyl. "Soup's on," he would say with a broad grin. He knew how much I hated the "soup" days. The smell of the stuff turned my stomach inside out. But it had to be done. All the parts had to gleam like new, then be meticulously checked before the engine was reassembled. Somehow I always managed to keep my breakfast down.'

The knowledge gained from her 'apprenticeship' proved invaluable during her flight. Her understanding of overhauling procedures was to save her engine on Bang

Biang Island, and enable her to continue with the flight.

Early in 1933 Mrs Bonney also finished a course in 'blind flying' with chief instructor Frank Gardiner of the Royal Queensland Aero Club. During the course she spent hours huddled in the rear cockpit of her aircraft beneath a small canvas tent-like hood. Unable to see out she learnt to fly her plane using only its flight instruments. To keep a constant height she had to carefully monitor her aircraft's altimeter and vertical aspect indicator. The latter was a glass tube and bubble contraption similar to a spirit level in appearance. Any slight variation and she had to correct her aircraft's nose attitude to hold the correct height.

A 'bat and ball' turn and balance indicator warned if the wings were not level or if the aircraft was skidding to either side. This instrument was also used in making turns. Direction was held by use of her aircraft compass. Compared with modern flight instruments, they were primitive and generally used only as a last resort if a pilot was caught unintentionally in a cloud or was forced to fly into one in an emergency.

Instrument flying demands absolute attention, rapid scanning of the various instruments, delicate handling of the aircraft's flying controls and the ability to disregard sensory illusions totally. When flying in cloud it is quite common for a pilot to get the feeling that he or she is in a turn, or even rolling upside down, when in fact the aircraft is flying straight and level. When this phenomenon occurs it is vital for the pilot to disregard 'the seat of the pants' and put complete faith in the instruments. If not, the aircraft will soon be out of control, frequently with fatal results!

Mrs Bonney had no intention of flying through cloud to England. Nor had she any intention of flying at night, unless it was absolutely necessary. However, she realised she could not risk attempting the flight without a sound knowledge of the art of blind flying. The weather in Europe and South-East Asia was notoriously unreliable and it was almost certain she would get caught in cloud at some stage. If she was forced to enter the dark, horizonless world of turbulence she was determined to come out the other side!

She also learnt how to take off and land in inky conditions. With only paraffin pot flares to guide her, she practised time after time on the Archerfield flarepath until she successfully mastered the skill. She could not afford to be caught in the air after last light, without any clue as to how to get down safely.

When she was not busy working or flying, Mrs Bonney was reading. During those months leading up to her flight, she read every book written by long distance flyers she could find. Alan Cobham and Francis Chichester had both written in great detail about their flights. Their books were invaluable. Both covered much of her intended route. Cobham and his navigator had flown a DH 50 floatplane from England to Australia and back, in 1926. In 1930 Chichester, flying an aircraft like hers, had become the second man to fly solo from England. Returning home via Japan his pioneer flying career came to an end when he was seriously injured in a crash at Katsuura.

Late in January 1933 Mrs Bonney was ready. She was competent in flying, navigating, servicing, blind flying and night flying, and she had a good grounding in meteorology. Her aircraft had been completely overhauled from prop to tail. Was it possible her husband Harry could find the smallest chink in her preparatory armour? She couldn't think of any. The time had come to find out. To her delight Harry Bonney couldn't think of any either.

'He was naturally very worried about the risks and took a great deal of persuading. But he realised that there was no valid objection on the grounds of ability or preparation. I had even planned menus and shopping lists for the housekeeper for the period I would be away. He knew how much I had set my heart on the flight and eventually agreed to it. He was a marvellous husband: kind and generous. From that moment he became totally involved.' In fact he did more than simply encourage and assist her, he agreed to pay all the bills. Mrs Bonney was not very successful in finding financial backers. The only sponsorship she obtained was from Lord Wakefield, whose company provided oil for the flight.

While making her preparations Lores Bonney received encouraging news. She had been awarded the Qantas Trophy for the most meritorious performance by a Queensland pilot during 1932. Her round-Australia flight had finally received official recognition.

On 26 January 1933 she wrote to the Department of Aviation for permission to make the flight to England. She gave her proposed itinerary and nominated 10 April as her departure date. She was just making the final preparations when she saw in the newspaper that another woman was considering the flight and was appealing for financial backing. In a flurry of anxiety she pushed ahead with her plans. Mrs Bonney knew that, given the unpredictable nature of wind and weather, and all the potential hazards associated with her aircraft, her chances of breaking the speed record would be a matter of luck. If she could do it, well and good, but no matter what, *she* would be the first woman to make the Australia-England flight. After all the training and all the preparations for the flight she had no intention of being pipped at the post.

My Little Ship was rapidly returned to the Qantas hangar to be specially modified for long distance operations. Extra fuel tanks were installed to increase the Moth's normal capacity of 80 litres to a total of 331 litres. A 168-litre tank occupied most of the space in the front cockpit, and the tiny baggage locker behind her seat held an 83-litre tank. With her engine consuming about 25 litres each hour, and cruising at 100 km/h she would have a range of 1300 kilometres. Her aircraft was normally capable of better speed but the lower estimate allowed for the drag caused by the extra equipment, and head winds.

It was not the first time her aircraft had been so equipped. Its previous owner, Flight Lieutenant C. W. Hill, had also installed extra fuel tanks for his famous race with Charles Kingsford Smith from England to Australia in 1930. Both were trying to break Bert Hinkler's record. However, as the two airmen approached Australia neck and neck, Hill crashed his aircraft at Kupang, Timor.

Mrs Bonney had a special instrument panel put in the cockpit to accommodate the extra equipment she required. She also installed an auxiliary oil tank to increase the engine's oil capacity by 5 litres. The Gipsy would burn more oil than normal on the long, hot legs over India and the Middle East. If the rate of oil consumption rose too much the normal capacity would be insufficient, and the engine would seize, with possibly fatal results.

At that time the American Aviation Department recommended all bush pilots to paint their aircraft a brilliant orange. It had been found to be invaluable by aerial searchers looking for lost aircraft. Mrs Bonney had both the upper and lower surfaces of her wings painted the bilious colour. If she was unfortunate enough to have an accident her aircraft would show up even if it turned over on the ground.

One problem that plagued all pilots of the biplane era was the fragility of their wooden propellers. Made of special wood, the graceful tapered blades had to be hand carved and finished by highly skilled craftsmen to the exact camber and pitch. It was essential that the blades be thin, especially towards the tips, if the rotary power of the engine was to be efficiently transferred into forward thrust. The penalty for this efficiency was fragility. The slightest contact with the ground, or a bird, would shatter them, while any prolonged friction caused by sand, hail or even heavy rain would wear them down to useless junk.

The flying books were littered with stories of lost records and shattered dreams as pilots languished beside their propeller-less aircraft in some remote outpost of the world. For before the days of international airlines, a new propeller could be months away by sea.

Mrs Bonney was determined not to fall into that trap. With the help of Arthur Baird, she had special straps fitted to the fuselage of her Moth to carry a spare propeller during the flight. The extra drag and resulting loss in airspeed would be a small price to pay for the added insurance of a spare.

Weight was the biggest problem. The question was

how to cram enough equipment and fuel in the little touring aircraft and not so reduce its performance that she could not take off from the numerous short strips she would encounter? During her round-Australia flight she had learned how altitude, temperature and weight exacted a crippling penalty on the Moth's ability to take off and climb.

'Weight had to be carefully checked, and my rations and clothes came in for a good deal of thought. For cold weather I decided on high boots, a pair of neck to ankle suede overalls, and a leather coat and helmet. For the tropics I had sandals, shorts, a wrap skirt to wear on landing, a blouse, a sun topee, a spine pad and sun goggles. The topee and spine pad I found a tremendous comfort.'

She avidly read every publication she could find dealing with survival. Her emergency equipment must be light but adequate to keep her alive for an extended period. Much of her route covered bleak, desolate country. If she crashed, help could be weeks away. She must be totally self-sufficient if she were to survive.

She put a great deal of thought and research into the final list. Everything was carefully packed and stowed in specially provided pockets in the two cockpits. And as each item was stowed away it was checked off. One forgotten item could be disastrous in an emergency: Dates, wheatmeal biscuits, chocolate, concentrated beef cubes, Ovaltine, bully beef, flask of brandy, two 7-litre cans of water, chewing gum, first aid kit, three boxes of compressed methylated spirits tablets, jack knife, and a revolver.

She also carried an inflatable rubber life raft lent by Qantas, and in her cockpit were a dozen message bags. These small weighted bags, with 2-metre-long red streamers attached, could be dropped to the ground with written notes inside.

As well as reading any book on long-distance flying that she could lay her hands on, Mrs Bonney also talked with every airman she could meet who had made the long flight. In her diary on 18 March she wrote, '. . . saw Charles

Ulm and Scotty Allan. They advise tankage not sufficient for Alor Star-Rangoon hop. Also wash out northern European route as country and conditions too treacherous. They advise Athens-Brindisi route.'

Their advice was to prove correct, and Mrs Bonney was later to regret not having taken it.

* * *

On the morning of 10 April 1933 she was ready. Her flight had been approved. *My Little Ship* was tuned to perfection. It stood awaiting her on the grass parking area at Archerfield, ready to return to the birthplace it had left three years earlier at the hands of Flight Lieutenant Hill. The forecast looked good. It was time to go.

A crowd had gathered to see her off. One of the last things she told Harry Bonney to try to allay his obvious anxiety was, 'If I am reported missing and nothing is heard of me for some time, don't worry. I will be down safely on the ground somewhere. With all my supplies I can hold out for a long time. Tell them to search along the coastline. Whenever possible I will be following the shore.'

She climbed into her tiny cockpit. The mechanic took hold of the propeller.

'Switches off?'

'Switches off,' she replied.

'Fuel on?'

'Fuel on.'

He swung the prop, slowly sucking fuel into the Gipsy's four cylinders.

'Switches on?'

'Switches on,' she replied, her excitement rising.

'Contact,' he said and swung the propeller sharply.

The engine fired, caught and sprang into life. Mrs Bonney taxied out, completed her final pre-flight check, waved quickly and then began her takeoff run. The heavily loaded Moth moved sluggishly at first. Then, gathering speed, the tail rose. She held the main wheels on the ground to gain extra flying speed, then slowly lifted off and climbed gently away. Harry Bonney watched the disappearing aircraft, a diminishing speck in the blue morning sky, until it was lost from sight.

The route she had chosen, even with her extended range, required twenty-eight refuelling stops. These were planned to be made at Charleville, Cloncurry, Camooweal, Darwin, Kupang, Lombok, Surabaya, Batavia, Singapore, Alor Star, Victoria Point, Rangoon, Calcutta, Allahabad, Jhansi, Jodhpur, Karachi, Jask, Bandar Abbas, Bushire, Basra, Baghdad, Aleppo, Konya, Constantinople, Sofia, Budapest, Frankfurt, with her final landing to be at London's Croydon airport. Timing for the speed record would begin as soon as she left Darwin.

At her first refuelling stop, Charleville hotelier Harry Corones presented her with a bottle of whisky to carry on the flight. This was his traditional gift for all pilots passing through on their way across the Timor Sea.

He added that to his knowledge none of the bottles had reached London intact. The usual practice was to take frequent nips to settle the nerves on the long lonely flight from Darwin to Kupang. The Timor crossing was the longest leg of the flight over water and one feared by airmen. An engine failure meant certain death. Several of the record breakers were said to have admitted to taking large doses of 'liquid courage'.

Next day she repeated the practice of her round-Australia trip and flew in company with Qantas aircraft to Daly Waters. As the mail plane descended to land, the pilots waved to each other and she peeled off in the direction of Darwin.

She reached the Northern Territory capital late on 13 April. She had already flown 3200 kilometres but had yet to leave Australia. From Darwin, she would be flying the recognised 'record' route. On her arrival the Brisbane *Courier Mail* reported

'Mrs Bonney was sighted over the racecourse at 4.40 p.m. and she landed ten minutes later. Messrs Langford Smith and Gordon Cowper went up to meet her, but missed her due to the poor visibility caused by bush fires.

'When a photographer asked her to pose she said,

"Don't take me, take the things I have brought. There's everything here except my kitchen stove and sewing machine." The aviatrix brought a large bundle of Brisbane newspapers which she distributed to those around the aeroplane. She was entertained last night by the local Shell representative.'

Mrs Bonney benefited from a full day's rest in Darwin while her aircraft was serviced. The next morning she was eager to make an early start across the Timor Sea. At 6.45 a.m. she was airborne. The Moth climbed slowly over the airport, leaving behind a small group of people who had gathered to see her off, and headed out to sea.

She was lucky to get away at all. But for the Reverend Keith Langford Smith she would have been stuck in Darwin. The flying minister had planned to accompany her as far as Melville Island, on his way to the Methodist Mission at Milingimbi in the Crocodile Islands. However, before they left, the mechanic had discovered a bad leak in the petrol line of *My Little Ship*. Without a moment's hesitation the minister had removed the line from his own aircraft *Sky Pilot*, and fitted it into *My Little Ship*.

'As I watched the Australian coast disappear I was very aware of the fact that there was not one island ahead between me and Timor 850 kilometres away,' Mrs Bonney recalls.

'I longed for something to break the monotony. Only once did I pass a bird. The night before I had marked off the whole crossing on my map. Every 120 kilometres I had pencilled in a small line corresponding with the distance I hoped to make each hour if the tail wind was as forecasted. Without any reference on the sea below I had no idea how I was actually doing. But to amuse myself I kept ticking off the kilometres as each hour passed. It gave me something to do and it became almost a game. I longed to cheat, just by five or ten minutes. The exercise gave me an understanding of some people's fascination for the solitary game of patience.

'Once or twice I was tempted to fly low and skim the water, to see if I could see any sharks, but I resisted the temptation and stayed up high. I made notes in my diary: "7 a.m. In the air. Very hazy. 7.15. A little clearer. 7.30. Pumping petrol. 7.40. Coming into very heavy haze. 8 a.m. One hour over water. Cross off first mark", etc.'

Occasionally she wondered about her inflatable boat. Would it be any use in the sea below if the worst happened? It was pretty crude by modern standards. According to press reports it was no more than '. . . a large omnibus inner tube, with a tin water bottle in the centre, held in place by a strip of black rubber.' The previous day it had been removed and checked. It was just as well for a large hole was discovered and the pump didn't work. It had been repaired but it wasn't reliable. Still it gave some feeling of security to know it was on board.

She had been over water for four-and-a-half hours when she noticed what appeared to be a dark cloud on the horizon. Apprehension turned to exhilaration when she realised it was the Timor coast. She was two hours ahead of time! She landed at Kupang having made the crossing in the fast time of five hours. Tail winds had helped but her average speed of 170 km/h was staggering nevertheless.

The next morning dawned hot and windless. The airfield was small. Her first attempt to take off failed. She could not get her heavy aircraft airborne and pulled up just in time. On the second attempt she pushed *My Little Ship* back to the very edge of the airfield, started up and quickly throttled on full power. As the far end of her run approached the Moth's wings seemed to clutch desperately at the still, hot air and the aircraft staggered off the ground with only centimetres to spare.

En route to Lombok she was disgusted to find that her husband's watch had been stolen from the cockpit. She had no way of telling the time, which was absolutely vital in aerial navigation. She would have to buy another at her next destination. Head winds forced her to change her plans and to land early on the beautiful island of Bali in search of fuel.

As she touched down on an emergency strip near Singaradja, the Balinese streamed in from all around to meet her. For half an hour confusion reigned supreme.

Nobody could speak a word of English. She was attempting to make them understand by sign language that she needed petrol, and was becoming more frustrated by the moment, when a huge car pulled up: it was the assistant governor. He told the airwoman that there was no hope of getting fuel until the next day and invited her to spend the night at the official residence.

That evening over dinner Governor Bulow tried to persuade her to remain the next day. They would arrange a special tiger hunt in her honour. Mrs Bonney regretted she could not do so and explained that she had a strict schedule to meet. She was still hoping to make a record time to England. Next morning there were further delays. It was the same old takeoff problem.

'I tried to get my machine into the air, without success. The long grass was the trouble. It was wing high and although I taxied backwards and forwards over it trying to flatten it down, it was useless. I made two abortive attempts to get off with grass flying in every direction, but soon realised it was dangerous. Mr Bulow ordered the natives to cut a track. This was done with a motor-drawn cutter they had brought to the field. It was fun, if not very comfortable, sitting up in the motor wagon, directing operations. There was a lot of laughter and shouted advice from the crowd who had arrived to watch my departure. When the track was finished it was as straight as the proverbial dog's hind leg.'

She was an hour-and-a-half behind schedule when she started the three-hour run to Surabaya. At Surabaya, she took on a maximum fuel load for the 700 kilometres to Batavia. Again she had trouble getting off. After two attempts, she finally staggered into the air. She landed at Batavia five-and-a-half hours later.

That night Mrs Bonney the pilot, gave way to Mrs Bonney the housewife as she wandered around the town's beautiful shops. She was fascinated with their displays of silk, batik, needlework, woven baskets, silver ornaments and jewellery. If only she had the time to shop and somewhere to stow her booty. But the airwoman quickly took control, as she remembered the takeoff problems.

She had her first taste of the savage monsoonal storms next day. As she approached Singapore she saw a huge black towering pall of cloud hanging over Muntok Island. The cascade of rain falling beneath it completely blotted out most of the island. Soon after she saw that her flight path was blocked by a line of similar storms. Low cloud forced her to fly only metres above the water. She hugged the coast and scurried on towards Singapore. All of a sudden the cloud above let go and she was in the midst of a downpour. She had no alternative but to open the throttle wide and carry on through it. Luckily she could still just make out the sea below. She could see nothing ahead.

As she passed out of the rain the airwoman was buffeted by violent turbulence and thrown around the cockpit. She was sure the wings would rip off.

Realising she was in the middle of a succession of storms, she made a series of changes to her course to avoid the forest of rain showers. In doing so she lost track of her position but eventually reached a clear patch.

'I saw a launch making its way towards an island. I wrote a note asking for direction, and threw it overboard in one of my message bags.

'They picked it up and the boat immediately altered course and pointed its bow in the direction of Singapore. I dipped my wings in thanks and flew in a straight line in the direction indicated. Eventually, coming out of a squall over a crowd of shipping, I saw Singapore ahead.'

That night she had a sumptuous dinner at the Raffles Hotel. She was tired. She had had her first taste of inhospitable weather, and was not looking forward to the next day's long journey over virgin forest. She decided to cheer herself up with one of the beautifully prepared fish entrees on the menu.

The following day she was ready to head off for Alor Star and Victoria Point. According to bulletins the weather was good all along the route. One more day's flying, she thought and she would be past the monsoonal belt of the inter-tropical front, and then there would be good weather all the way — well, as far as Europe anyway.

She was at Singapore's Seletar airport early. She felt a little seedy but was sure the dull uncomfortable feeling would pass. However, as she was walking over to her aircraft with the Shell representative she suddenly felt desperately ill. Something was seriously wrong, she felt dizzy and bilious, and her temperature was rising dramatically. There was no way she was going to be able to fly.

A doctor was called and Mrs Bonney returned to the Raffles. A few minutes later she had the verdict — fish poisoning — Why the devil had she had that fish the previous night? She should have known better.

'This unlucky day caused me the loss of any chance of a record and was the beginning of my troubles. Had I gone through that day I would have had ideal flying conditions. Next day the monsoon broke and I was forced to land on the beach of Bang Biang Island.'

5
Bang Biang Island

MRS BONNEY MISSING
NO NEWS OF AUSTRALIAN FOR TWO DAYS
LAST REPORTED FLYING OVER ALOR STAR IN MALAYA

These were the headlines Western Australians read as they opened their morning newspapers at the breakfast tables on 22 April. All around the country there were similar headlines. Till then her flight had excited little interest from the nation's press. Record of her safe arrival and departure at refuelling points had been tucked away in little paragraphs on the inside pages. Now she was suddenly front page news.

Reports stated that she had not been heard of since passing over Alor Star two days earlier. They spoke of growing concern for her safety.

'Aerodrome officials at Rangoon know nothing of the reason for her nonappearance there,' the Western Australian daily reported. The weather for the last few days has not been ideal for flying, and Burma has received indications that the monsoon has arrived.'

In Brisbane Harry Bonney remained outwardly calm on hearing the news. So far away and with communications so poor with the Malay Peninsula he could do little but wait it out. He received great comfort from her parting advice, 'If I am reported missing and nothing is heard of me for some time, don't worry. I will be down safely on the ground somewhere.' But no doubt, deep down, he was churning with anxiety.

Besieged by reporters he finally made a statement.

'I can't imagine that there is anything wrong with my

wife. She would be so busy after her flight to Alor Star and she wouldn't arrive there until between 5 p.m. and 6 p.m. She would not have had time to cable me having so much to attend to.'

It seemed that he had chosen to disbelieve or ignore the steady stream of reports coming in from Singapore. He simply decided to say, to the press at any rate, that his wife was not missing. This saved having to answer any more searching questions that might pierce the guard he had placed on his emotions. They were a personal matter not to be splashed all over the front pages.

From a further remark it would appear that the gentlemen of the press and Harry Bonney did not really see eye to eye and he did not welcome their attention.

'I am surprised that the Australian newspapers did not make better arrangements to follow up my wife's flight. If the papers want good news they should be prepared to pay for it. The arrangements concerning my wife's flight seem to have been very poor indeed and it is not as though the news had been tied up in any way.'

Unlike the previous round-Australia flight, Mrs Bonney had not given exclusive publishing rights to any one paper for the story of her flight.

He concluded his interview by stating again that he was not at all worried by the reports coming in from overseas. He believed she was just running late.

The RAF detachment at Singapore did not share the Brisbane businessman's confidence. The RAF commanding officer at Seletar took control. The military were the only organisation with equipment and facilities necessary for a major search of the area. He sent messages to all aerodromes south of Rangoon and all shipping in the area to be on the lookout. An air force seaplane was despatched to the area to scour the coastline and the scores of small islands off the mainland.

On the third day it had become obvious, even to her husband, that Mrs Bonney was down somewhere along the Burma coast. Newspapers carried the headlines, 'Great RAF Search For Mrs Bonney. Little Hope After Three Days Silence.'

Her friends found little comfort in the ensuing report.

'Silence . . . which means there is still no news of Mrs Bonney, cousin of the ill-fated Bert Hinkler . . . the first woman to atttempt the Australia-England flight is somewhere between Alor Star and Victoria Point.

'Perhaps forced down on the coast she may at this moment be stranded in the small collapsible boat off the coast of Burma, still alive but with hope fast fading. On the other hand fate may have stepped in already, a wrecked plane may be lying in the jungle — and one of the most treacherous sections of the world's air routes have claimed yet another victim.'

The report went on to recall that only a week earlier the Italian pilot Robiano had gone down somewhere near Victoria Point on a flight from England to Australia. A wrecked aircraft containing a body, believed to be the Italian, had since been found.

Indeed there was little to promote the cause of aviation in the papers on 23 April 1933. It had been a bad week. Around the world, airlines were still struggling for financial security. The public had been slow to accept the new form of transportation. Many were yet to be convinced that air travel was safe. For every successful long-distance record flight, the man in the street seemed to read of half a dozen who did not make it. Unfortunately then, as today, it was the disasters that received the biggest headlines.

Sharing the news with Mrs Bonney were three other missing flyers. Besides the Italian, whose death was confirmed a few days later, New Zealand aviatrix Jean Batten, and English flyer Captain Bill Lancaster were also long overdue.

Jean Batten was attempting to break Amy Johnson's England-Australia record and had been missing for three days between Persia and India. She later turned up in Karachi, on the back of a lorry. She had damaged her aircraft landing on a plateau near Baluchistan. Baluchi tribesmen later rescued her and took her to the nearest town, Las Bela, where officials put her on a truck for Karachi.

Bill Lancaster was down somewhere in the middle of the Sahara Desert. The English pilot was flying Charles Kingsford Smith's *Southern Cross Minor* from London to Cape Town in an attempt to break the record that was also held by Amy Johnson. Lancaster was well known in Australia. In 1928 he had flown out from England while Hinkler was making his epic solo flight. But unlike Hinkler, Lancaster had not been alone. He had carried Mrs Jessie Miller of Melbourne who became the first woman passenger to make the trip. The Englishman had disappeared on the day Mrs Bonney had reached Darwin, after taking off from Reggan. On the same day one newspaper was suggesting little hope of finding the Queensland woman, it also reported that the fruitless search for Lancaster was being abandoned. His mummified body was found alongside the skeleton of his aircraft by a French Army patrol in 1962. A pitiful diary recorded his death from thirst.

* * *

While the press speculated on the fate of the airwoman, Mrs Bonney spent three days of drama and despair on Bang Biang Island. It was her innate sense of humour that prevented her from wallowing in misery and self pity. As events unfurled after she reached the beach, the stranded pilot found herself involved in a situation that continually reminded her of a Charlie Chaplin comedy.

She had been sitting for a long time watching the surf pounding her overturned aircraft when she realised that the tide was coming in. Soon there would be little more than matchwood to collect. Already her equipment was being washed out of the cockpit and was floating in to shore.

It was growing dark and the buffaloes were moving back towards the bush. There was not a soul in sight. The only noise was the pounding surf and the far off rumble of thunder in the direction of Victoria Point.

She remembered having seen a settlement from the air, so decided to go and find help. Now over the initial shock of the crash, she was thinking ahead again. If she could get *My Little Ship* out of the water and up off the beach it might still be repairable. She would need a score of helpers to help her beat the tide and nightfall.

As Mrs Bonney stood and turned towards the bush she saw a crowd of villagers watching from the shelter of the trees. Her troubles were over! There stood her aircraft rescue team. All she had to do was get them to help her, and that should not be too difficult.

She hurried towards them beckoning. As she moved closer she noticed they were dressed in a motley assortment of clothes; some were bare chested with sarongs, others wore ill-fitting European-style trousers and tattered shirts, while the children were naked. They did not appear friendly, in fact some looked hostilely at the approaching airwoman. She slowed down, suddenly unsure of her reception. She felt the pocket of her flying suit for the comfort of the revolver her husband had given her for the flight. It was not there. It must have fallen out in the crash. She dug into the other pocket for her jack knife. It too was missing.

'I returned to my plane to search for them. But this was difficult as I had to grope around with my eyes shut and holding my breath under the water. I spent some time trying to find them in the sand beneath the upturned cockpit for I felt quite unprotected without them and was really worried that the natives were hostile. I couldn't find them and eventually decided there was nothing for it but to go back towards them and hope for the best.'

As she walked towards them the whole crowd started to back away. Then to her amazement they turned and retreated. What she had taken to be sullen hostility was, in fact, fear. To a man, they were scared of the tiny white woman in her strange flying outfit! The faster she walked, the faster they retreated. Mrs Bonney could have found the episode amusing, but she became exasperated with their timidity. Every minute wasted meant the tide was getting a little higher. She needed their help.

To stem their retreat she stood still and beckoned with both hands, at the same time attempting to smile through her weariness and discouragement. They continued to retreat looking back over their shoulders. Eventually one stood his ground. She walked slowly up to him praying he wouldn't lose his nerve. Bewildered, but apparently sure he had nothing to fear in the strange looking white woman who had arrived so unceremoniously from the air, the man allowed Mrs Bonney to take him by the arm. Slowly and very gently she led him over towards the wreck. Realising he could not understand a word she said, the airwoman pointed at the plane then patted the sand. He understood at once and returned to the crowd.

After a quick conference during which he rapped out some orders, the whole group rushed down the beach and into the surf. From where Mrs Bonney stood it was a strange sight. Silhouetted against the setting sun the people climbed all over the Moth. Some were already walking on the inverted fuselage and others were trying to clamber onto the wings. They were shouting and gesticulating wildly. If they weren't quickly organised, Mrs Bonney thought, they would do more damage to the fabric and wood super-structure than the waves.

She rushed in among them shouting and waving them off the aircraft. By demonstration and sign language she showed them where to hold the aircraft. After an immense amount of straining, it was obvious that they would not be able to lift the waterlogged machine. The water trapped inside doubled its weight. It would not budge. Meanwhile, more islanders had gathered on the shore. Mrs Bonney beckoned the men among them to help. They bounded into the water. The aircraft moved a little then stuck again.

'Then I had a brainwave. If I could get them to exert their concerted energy as each wave rolled in, maybe the surge of water would help. I invented a sort of sailor's "Heave Ho" chant, at the same time expressing great exertion as the next wave came in. They quickly grasped the idea and with me chanting and raising my arms in exertive expression, wave by wave, they slowly inched *My Little Ship* towards the shore.

'I will never forget the sight. It was nearly dark except

for a rim of light on the horizon. As they worked, they turned their heads to watch for each incoming wave, and the whites of their eyes became accentuated, gleaming in the near dark. My nerves overtaxed by the last few hours were near breaking point and I found the effect very frightening.'

Eventually the aircraft was dragged on to the beach above the high tide mark. It was still wrong way up, but it was pitch dark and Mrs Bonney was exhausted. The rest could wait till morning. Gathering a few sodden clothes and her brandy flask she indicated to the natives that she was ready to follow them.

The procession walked in single file towards lights that twinkled through the jungle. When they reached the little village she was met by a tiny woman who led her through a spiked bamboo enclosure to a palm leaf thatched hut on stilts. Her guide motioned for her to climb the bamboo ladder to the doorway.

As she entered the smoke-filled interior, Mrs Bonney recoiled at the nauseating odour of bad fish. Dozens of villagers were squatting on the woven mat floor staring intently at their unexpected guest.

'I was standing watching the strange scene in front of me when a little brown hand crept into mine. My diminutive guide then led me by the hand into a small semi-partitioned room just off the entrance and indicated that this particular spot was mine.

'She gazed at me with large sorrowful eyes that expressed such a depth of sympathy that I came close to tears. She noticed that my hand was bleeding rather badly and, moaning softly, she tenderly held it to her face.

'From that moment on she became my shadow, a self-appointed bodyguard. She would allow no one else to do anything for me. If they attempted it, she would wave her arms and let go with a cascade of words, all the time putting herself protectively between me and the culprit. My bodyguard would not relax until they moved right back and kept a safe distance. Then she would trot back to my side.

'I nicknamed her SOS, short for Soul of Sympathy.

During the four days I was marooned on the island, she did everything humanly possible to distract my mind and make me happy.'

Mrs Bonney's slashed hand was becoming very, very painful. The gash across the knuckles was deep. The last thing she needed with all her other troubles was a poisoned hand.

Too tired to return to her aircraft for the first aid kit, she searched for some other method of sterilising the wound. Coming from another partitioned section of the hut were great clouds of smoke. That must be the 'kitchen', she thought. Suspended over the fire was a cooking pot and a brass urn of boiling water. She filled a small bowl, took it back to her quarters and bathed the wound. One of the few possessions she had brought from the wreck was the bottle of whisky from the hotel in Charleville. It was still sealed. She had felt no need to imbibe on the way across the Timor. She carefully opened the bottle and poured some of its antiseptic contents into the wound. Disregarding the searing pain, she covered the wound with a handkerchief.

She was able to make SOS understand that she wanted to put on dry clothes. She had removed her sodden leather flying boots when her friend returned with a brand new native sarong. Dozens of curious eyes watched her every move. To their surprise, rather than wear the native dress, she pinned it to a line that she made with her long flying boot laces. Behind the instant room divider she was able to change into clothes which had fortunately remained dry in her canvas grip.

To escape the hut's sickening odour and the stifling heat she moved over to the entrance and sat with her feet on the ladder watching swarms of fireflies light up the night.

After going over the day's events, she decided to try and find out how far away the nearest white settlement was.

'I went back into the hut and placed my hand alongside that of one of the natives. I drew his attention to the different colour of our skins, and using signs tried to find out if there were people with skins like mine nearby. After a long pantomime he seemed to understand. He smiled and made signs indicating that white people were a long way away.

'I knew that I could be no more than 30 or 40 miles from Victoria Point and decided to try and get a message through. I had a pencil with me and searched through my few possessions for a piece of paper. The natives obviously realised I wanted to write, and to my amazement brought me a pen, ink and paper. I found they could write and this was decidedly comforting.'

She wrote a long note recording the day's events, saying she had sufficient emergency rations for three weeks, was being well treated by the natives and was reasonably comfortable. She had already decided to live off her survival rations rather than take food from the islanders. She feared understandably that her system might not take to their food. She had enough worries without getting ill. Unless her rations ran out before she was rescued she would stick to the 'hard tack'.

The only information she could not send to her would-be rescuers was her exact position. She decided to see if any of the circle crowded around her could identify their island from her map.

'The map was the one I had been using at the time of my crash and gave a list of the names of all the islands in Siamese and English. I read out the names of the islands to them. At first they just shook their heads but as I went on they became interested. To my delight when I came to Koh Jang (Saddle Island) and Koh-Pha-Yam (Deslisle Island), they nodded vigorously and pointed. I soon managed to find out that I was not on the mainland at all but on Bang Biang Island.'

She finished off her note and held it out for someone to take. The men drew back. She decided it was the time for positive action so selecting her victim she took him by the arm, handed him the note and gently pushed him out of the door. He went only as far as the bottom of the ladder, stopped and stood silently staring up at the airwoman.

Either he had no wish to go trekking through the jungle on her behalf, or he was scared of the dark.

Whatever the case, Mrs Bonney quickly realised that some sort of bribe was needed. To wait till next morning would mean a loss of half a day, and her husband would be worried enough already. She must get news of her safety to civilisation as quickly as possible.

She fetched the watch she had purchased to replace the gold one that had been stolen at Kupang. It had already been much admired by a number of islanders. She snatched back the note from the hand of her reluctant courier. Placing the watch on top of the note and standing on tip-toe the airwoman turned slowly, offering it to the men who now clustered around her.

For several minutes no one moved. They chattered among themselves, then finally one came forward reluctantly and took them from her. He moved slowly to the door and hesitantly down the ladder. With impatient words and gestures she told him to get a move on! He looked back wistfully at the hut as he walked slowly into the inky darkness.

Mrs Bonney was to find out later that it was a minor miracle to induce an islander to travel at night. He must have been very brave, for the jungle was full of wild animals and his only weapon was a long knife. Her courier must have paddled to the mainland and walked all night to reach his destination.

Confident that she would soon be rescued the Australian now relaxed. She returned inside the hut and sat down with the islanders. She smiled and nodded to the thirty men and women squatted around her. This obviously met with their approval as they grinned back and, wagging their heads, chattered to her.

With SOS sitting beside her, she watched as women placed several shallow wooden platters on the floor. On them were sweet-smelling tobacco leaves, pieces of dried maize leaves, a tin containing a pink paste, green leaves resembling mulberry leaves, betel nuts, and a tool for chipping the nuts.

She watched fascinated as the betel nut chewing ceremony began. Everyone selected their favourite brand of leaf, smeared it with the pink paste, rolled it up and popped it in their mouths. This was quickly followed with a piece of betel nut. There was much chewing and even more spitting.

At first she avoided the sight — it was not quite drawing room behaviour at gatherings of the Brisbane social set — yet it became obvious that to her hosts it was as normal and correct as taking a drink or lighting a cigarette at a formal European party.

As she overcame her reserve she became totally absorbed by their knack of spitting through the clear spaces in the floor. The bamboo canes were laid about 2 centimetres apart. Long streams of crimson fluid shot from their mouths straight through the narrow openings and no one ever missed. The floor was not marked anywhere.

Mrs Bonney remembered that she had copied some Malay phrases out of Francis Chichester's book. She found her 'emergency' note book and tried them out on the gathering.

'Saja minta mata-mata,' she said, meaning, 'I want a policeman.' To her delight they nodded vigorously, so she carried on. As the evening progressed she had learnt the names of a number of items around the hut.

Before she settled down for her first night on the island she took a couple of aspirin and a good dose of whisky. Her head was still aching as a result of the knock during the crash.

During the night she awoke to hear loud voices in the hut. Momentarily she was petrified. Only half awake she almost convinced herself that it had all been a bad dream. But then she was aware of the pain in her hand. It was true. She lay in despair and, as the voices continued, she became increasingly worried. She could stand it no longer. She lifted her sari curtain and walked into their midst. They were all hunched around one of the men as he laboriously wrote a letter. When they saw her they burst into broad smiles. As she settled down again she was ashamed of her mistrust of these kindly people. The letter, in fact, was to their district officer telling him of Mrs Bonney's arrival and asking him to come to see her.

Next morning she was up early and went straight to the

aircraft. It was a heart-breaking sight. The wings were badly damaged and were probably beyond repair. The fin and rudder were a crumpled mass, the propeller was shattered and the fuselage and engine, though outwardly undamaged, had taken in litres of salt water. There was no hope of quick repairs. The Moth would need to be completely rebuilt and that would be exceedingly difficult.

She managed to dismantle the wings before the oppressive heat forced her to head for the shade. The next job would be to turn *My Little Ship* upright on the undamaged undercarriage. But that would have to wait for the cool of the late afternoon.

Back in the shelter of the hut she rigged up a line and hung out her maps to dry. All her equipment was around her. She decided to turn her quarters into some semblance of home. She might have a long stay. An hour later she was satisfied with her 'boudoir'. She had a dressing table made of ration tins covered with bright silk. On it, in a wooden tray, stood a mirror, powder and hairbrush. She ran out of tins before she could make a washstand, and had to content herself with a large bowl on the floor. A tin lid made a soap tray and her toothbrush was stuck through the bamboo matting.

Her domestic chores over, Mrs Bonney realised she had not eaten since her refuelling stop at Alor Star twenty hours ago. Even then she had only had a few biscuits chewed while supervising the pumping of petrol. She made a sumptuous meal of biscuits, cheese, and dates from her rations, swilled down with a steaming cup of Ovaltine.

With bright daylight streaming in the entrance of the hut she was able to see where its awful odour came from. Strung along the high ceiling were row upon row of dried fish. Among the varieties she saw huge stingrays, which she found out later were considered a great delicacy.

Following a midday sleep she was taken on a tour of the cool jungle close to the village. Her guide, the ever present SOS, smiled with delight as she led her charge hand in hand along a track followed by a crowd of curious onlookers. They reached a small clearing and sat down. Within minutes they were surrounded by scores of monkeys playing in the trees and swinging on vines. The bird-loving Australian was also fascinated by the birds, particularly one, a huge black and white creature, which made an uncanny whining sound as it flapped its wings.

Late in the day she led a working party of men back to the aircraft. They rolled the Moth right way up and wheeled it close to the hut. There Mrs Bonney put to good use the knowledge she had painstakingly gained with the engineers during her Qantas 'apprenticeship'.

'I removed the petrol tank and emptied the contents into any vessel which would hold the precious fluid. Sand was lodged in every conceivable space and I had to dig and scrape it away before washing the engine down.'

Aware of the corrosive effect of the salt water she drained the oil sump and coated the whole engine and ancillary equipment with oil. She removed the spark plugs and filled each cylinder. With any luck it would act as an antidote to the cancerous spread of rust inside the 'mirror finished' cylinder walls and to the meticulously matched pistons and rings. Before she returned inside the hut for the night she had built a huge bonfire, ready to light if a searching aircraft flew overhead.

That evening she added a little rice from the family rice bowl to her beef tea — much to her hosts' delight. She had really become one of the family. She gathered with them in the communal living area and spent a happy evening adding to her Malay vocabulary.

She had been in bed some time when she heard a great commotion outside. The women were rushing around tidying up the hut and the men had all hurried outside. Looking out she saw a small group of people arrive followed by men carrying baskets and bundles.

The leader stepped forward and in broken English introduced himself as Khum Ranong Rae, the district officer. He had received the letter the villagers had so laboriously written the previous night, and had come to help her. He had brought his wife and the district opium inspector with him.

The two officials cut quite a picture in comparison with the islanders. The inspector looked very dapper in his wide-legged black satin trousers. He also wore a spotless, well fitting, military cut jacket of white duck; white canvas slippers; and a white topee. The opium inspector wore khaki shorts, a short tight jacket, which Mrs Bonney was sure would burst at any minute, and a little hat similar to those worn by Alpine climbers. He smoked a long thin cigar incessantly and laughed almost non-stop. Khum's wife wore a beautiful sarong and stunning gold jewellery. Also in the party were their children. They were naked.

The visitors presented Mrs Bonney with baskets full of tinned food. Canned pineapple, cream, coffee, fish, meat, biscuits and tea. Khum immediately opened a number of them and invited her to tuck in. Evidently he was under the impression that she was starving. Probably the natives had thought, on the previous night when she ate nothing, that the airwoman had no food with her. She pounced on a tin of pineapple.

While she ate, the district officer explained that he had sent word to Rangoon the moment he received the villagers' letter. He and his party would remain 'until the white people arrived'.

That night when she settled down again on her matting bed she was virtually alone in the hut. Khum had moved her admiring public out and only SOS and a couple of others remained. As had become her custom she lit a mosquito coil by the bed, not that there were any around, but to dull the ever-present fish odour. Things looked brighter and she was already wondering if somehow she might still continue with the flight.

Next day she gave *My Little Ship* another going over with the remainder of the oil. She also used up every last drop from her grease gun. There was nothing more she could do. She got out her camera and spent the day recording the whole scene on film.

She was still stalked by a curious crowd watching her every move. With her food problem no longer critical she decided to give them a treat. Dipping into the emergency supplies she pulled out a box of chocolate bars. It was time to repay a little of their kindness. They had frequently brought her little presents such as jungle fruits, bananas, coconuts, betel nuts and dried fish! SOS always took the gift, sent the giver on his way with a withering look, then rearranged it on a platter and presented it to Mrs Bonney.

The airwoman divided the chocolate and handed it to the natives who had grouped around. She had trouble containing her laughter when she watched what took place.

'They took it and very carefully unfolded the silver paper. They smelled the paper and smiled, then held it under the noses of those who sat nearby so that they might enjoy it also. Then they tasted the silver paper, but it did not come up to their expectations. Then remembering the contents which they had overlooked, they turned it over in their fingers, and eyed the sticky mess with deep suspicion.

'They looked across at me enquiringly so I began to feed myself with imaginary pieces of chocolate. They were not taking any chances, however, and took tiny nibbles. Later however it became a case of hiding my chocholate.'

The same ceremony occurred when she introduced them to the wonders of chewing gum.

On the third day she and Khum were walking near the hut when the official stopped, listened intently and said, 'Motor boat.' He pointed in the direction he believed the sound came from, but Mrs Bonney could hear nothing.

When they reached the hut he quietly told his group to pack their things and departed as simply as they had come.

'I would have liked to reward him, but money was refused, saying he was an officer. Khum gave me to understand that he had only done his duty. I was so impressed with his sincerity and simple dignity, and touched by his kindness to me, that on my arrival in London I wrote to the Governor of Ranong, telling him of Khum's kindness and also of the care the natives had taken of me.'

About half an hour after the district officer and his party departed two boats arrived. On board were a New Zealander named Aitken, employed by the Siamese Tin Syndicate and a jovial Scot, called J. W. Petrie, of the Bangram Tin Syndicate. They explained how an exhausted native had brought her letter to them at the mine after travelling on foot for a day. They listened to her story then reassured her that they had immediately sent news out that she was alive and well.

That night they held a hilarious party in Palm Leaf Cottage as she had named the hut. They tucked into a hamper the miners had brought, which included plenty of 'liquid refreshment'. 'Our table was a box, our illumination a hurricane lamp, and our dress suited the temperature, but the Savoy never saw a gayer party,' Mrs Bonney recalled.

6
Overhaul in India

LOST AIRWOMAN FOUND IN ISLAND JUNGLE
CRASH LANDING IN STORM   CRASH DUE TO BUFFALO
LIVING ON SHORT RATIONS   LEARNING MALAY
LIFESAVING DASH WITH FOOD   AMAZING PLUCK
RESCUED BY RAF FLYING BOAT
WILL REPAIR PLANE ON ISLAND   MAY GO ON WITH FLIGHT

The newspapers had a heyday when the news flashed out from Singapore across the United Press Association electric telegraph. Sub-editors across the country dashed off the headlines which did not always bear any resemblance to the facts. However, the story made exciting reading and that was what sold newspapers.

Despite inaccuracies and wild conjecture perpetrated by journalists attempting to build their stories around sketchy details, the news was good. Harry Bonney was relieved but publicly, 'not surprised'. He had said all along there was nothing to worry about, that she would be down safe somewhere.

For her parents in Wangaratta the news was just what the doctor ordered. Since his daughter had disappeared Norbert Rubens had been ill in bed. His doctor had diagnosed a severe nervous complaint caused by worry over his daughter's whereabouts. A reporter from the *Sun* phoned the Rubens with the good news. Mrs Rubens rushed to her husband's side to tell him. When she returned minutes later she said he had shown signs of recovering already.

On the morning of her fourth day on Bang Biang Island, Mrs Bonney was preparing to leave. It had been decided the previous evening to take the aircraft to Victoria Point in a large sampan with the two Tin Syndicate launches. If they were lucky they would get there in time to catch the S.S. *Juna* which was leaving that day for Rangoon.

Under the guidance of the two miners, fifty islanders had worked all night dismantling the de Havilland and had carried the parts through the jungle to a beach at the back of the island. On their orders Mrs Bonney had gone to bed. When she awoke at dawn the job was complete. The dismantled aircraft was on the beach waiting to be loaded onto the sampan.

Before she left Palm Leaf Cottage for the last time Mrs Bonney looked around for SOS. She was nowhere to be found. The previous night Mrs Bonney had given her companion all the silver coins she could find among her few personal belongings, and with the aid of drawings she had made the Malay girl understand that she was to make a necklace of the coins. SOS had been delighted with the gift but the sparkle was missing from her smile and tears had welled in her eyes when they left each other to go to bed. She knew her friend was leaving the island. Obviously rather than have Mrs Bonney witness her grief at the final parting, Soul of Sympathy had gone quietly into the jungle and would not return until the launch had departed. They never met again.

Departure was delayed an hour while the group waited for the rising tide to free the launches from the muddy bottom. They finally struggled across tangled mangrove roots that lined a small river and boarded the boats. The boats and the sampan were poled down river to deeper water and the sampan was joined by a rope to one of the launches. When they reached safe water the motors were started and they headed out to sea and Victoria Point.

They were an hour behind and would have to race if they were to arrive before the *Juna* left. Mrs Bonney had much on her mind. She felt great sadness at leaving her friends on the island. She would never forget their kindness and understanding. At the same time she was already thinking ahead. They must reach Victoria Point in time to catch the boat. It would be three weeks before it returned. Three weeks waiting to get to Rangoon to see if her aircraft could be repaired.

All of a sudden it had become her goal to get *My Little Ship* back in the air. The plan was already forming. There was no longer any hope of bettering Amy Johnson's record time between the two countries, but she still could be the first woman to make the flight westwards to England. The records had always been made coming from England with the prevailing tail winds. Her flight had been planned the hard way — into the wind. She might not be the fastest, but what did that really matter? She would be first. All she had to do was repair that wreck of an aircraft bobbing along on the sampan 20 metres behind in their wake. It wouldn't be the first time a flight had been completed in a plane rebuilt on the way. The Australians, Parer and McIntosh, had crashed and rebuilt their biplane three times before reaching Australia in the great 1919 air race.

The indomitable will that had punctuated her transition from bored housewife to commercial pilot was again in charge. The despair that had overwhelmed her on the beach at Bang Biang was gone. Though still sitting at the stern of the pitching launch, with the wreck of *My Little Ship* in tow, Mrs Bonney was already dreaming of the two of them cruising high above India, bound for London.

* * *

Captain le Britton, Master of the S.S. *Juna,* watched from the bridge as the last of his passengers came aboard. He would be glad to get away. The sun was already high and with no breeze the heat was stifling. Once out to sea he could relax a little and undo the top buttons of his damned high necked uniform tunic. If only the paragons of tradition and etiquette of the British merchant marine sailed this steamy corner of the world for a while they would soon change the rules, he thought.

The deck crew had raised the gangway. He leaned out

over the open wing of the bridge. A muffled order from the deck and the mooring lines went snaking across the water to waiting hands on the dock. In the wheelhouse the helmsman was at his post. He must remember to post a couple of extra lookouts once they left Victoria Point, he thought. That signal the radio officer received the day before had said that a woman pilot was missing in the area and might be on one of the hundreds of islands they would pass on the voyage to Rangoon. Secretly he didn't fancy her chances of getting down in one piece on most of those craggy islands.

'Slow ahead. Starboard fifteen,' he called. The clang of the ship's telegraph and its answering signal from the engine room was quickly followed by the steady quickening beat of the ship's engine. It was not so much a sound as a beat he could feel through his feet from the deck.

As the S.S. *Juna* got slowly under way, the Captain's attention was drawn to an approaching launch. Its occupants were standing and waving madly. He could see a white woman in a topee who seemed so excited in her efforts to attract their attention that she almost fell overboard. Some distance astern of the scurrying boat he could see another tiny steam launch towing a sampan carrying a strange looking load. He could swear that was a pair of aircraft wheels sticking up in the air.

'Good heavens it *is* a wrecked aeroplane,' he said to himself.

'Stop engines. Wheel amidships.' Moments later the anchor dropped with a rattle and splash.

Mrs Bonney had been first to see the ship. When Port Victoria first came into sight nearly an hour earlier, she had noticed a thick coil of smoke which soon had become recognisable as the coastal steamer approaching Victoria Point. By the time the slow-moving launches were nigh on Port Victoria the *Juna* had taken on her passengers and was ready to leave. In a race against time the Scottish miner, Petrie, opened the throttle wide, and the second launch towing *My Little Ship* dropped well astern.

They were still a kilometre away when a great belch of

smoke from the steamer's tall funnel told them she was underway. Petrie swung the wheel and took up a course to intercept the *Juna* as she headed out to sea.

An hour later Mrs Bonney and her aircraft were safely on board. Using the ship's derrick, sweating lascars had manhandled the Moth aboard and the sad looking collection of aircraft bits and pieces stood on the foredeck.

It was time to say goodbye to her two friends. Together they drank a farewell toast from her bottle of Scotch whisky. The two men autographed the bottle, and then returned to their launches. As the two moved slowly away from the ship's side waving goodbye and good luck, Mrs Bonney felt strangely sad. Once again she was among strangers. It was odd to think that only twenty-four hours beforehand the two tin miners had also been total strangers. It wasn't the length of time you knew people, but the experiences you shared that count, she thought.

The voyage to Rangoon took three days. She didn't waste a moment of the time. When not on deck taking a breather she was below in the workshop overhauling her Gipsy engine. The chief engineer spent hours helping her totally dismantle the motor. Every single tiny part was laid out on the bench, just as she had done at Archerfield. Every part was washed in kerosene. Sand had found its way into the engine everywhere. When they lifted the cylinders, litres of salt water flowed onto the hot steel deck. The heat was stifling and she was forced to take frequent breaks to cool off. While on deck she watched the islands between Tavoy and Rangoon slip by. Few appeared to have any beach at all and many were no more than jungle encrusted crags erupting out of the water. Thank heavens for the beach at Bang Biang, she thought.

She spent one evening writing a long letter to her husband putting down in detail the events that led up to her crash landing and her adventures on the island. When it arrived in Brisbane weeks later, Harry Bonney released long extracts to the press so that the facts could be published. The next day the Brisbane *Courier Mail* devoted half a page to the account. Commenting on her report the journalist wrote:

'The long letter not only shows courage, but an infinite resource in the face of disaster . . . Disappointment is manifest throughout the letter, which has, however, no hint of self pity, but a poignant regret that the misfortune might minimise her husband's confidence in her skill as a pilot, and sorrow at the damage to "my beloved *Little Ship*".'

'It is strange how man plans and God disposes,' Mrs Bonney wrote, summing up her misadventure.

As the *Juna* approached Rangoon the airwoman was busy repacking her few belongings and the emergency supply kit.

'On the island I had given the natives some of my chewing gum tablets. They were a great success and were considered a very special treat. While packing I discovered that every single pack of chewing gum was missing. But also my boxes of methylated spirits were gone. It didn't take long to figure the reason. The tiny portable cooking tablets looked just like chewing gum. The natives had eaten both! I was quite worried at first, but when I remembered some of the food I had seen them eat, I decided that the metho tablets would be child's play to their digestion.'

At Victoria Point she had cabled Harry Bonney asking him what he wished her to do next. Should she continue or should she return home? She knew what she wanted to do but the expense of repairing her aircraft required his approval. She prayed that her husband had not lost faith in her ability.

At Rangoon she received his reply, 'Leaving it in your hands.' She was riding a high until the Italian consular officer, Carlo Minto, brought her back down with a thud.

Signor Minto, an Italian Air Force officer, had written to Mrs Bonney after hearing reports that she was *en route* to Rangoon in the *Juna*. He mentioned having arranged repairs to the damaged aircraft of German airwoman Eli Beinhorn at Rangoon a year before, and offered to do the same for her. Mrs Bonney had eagerly accepted the invitation.

On her arrival he inspected the wrecked de Havilland,

then turned to the airwoman and sadly shook his head. It was beyond the repair facilities of Rangoon. Her only hope was to get it to the workshops of the Indian Air Survey Company in Calcutta. It would need to be totally rebuilt. Officials in Calcutta might just be able to get hold of the new parts required.

At this moment nobody would have blamed the stranded flyer if she had forgotten the whole idea and gone home. The whole business seemed hopeless. Other and more famous flyers had given up with less reason. But not the unbeatable Lores Bonney. No way was she going home, except via England! When the Rangoon-Calcutta mail steamer *Arakola* sailed next day the airwoman and *My Little Ship* were on board.

She had noticed a reference to her heavily bandaged hand in the Rangoon paper that morning. As people recognised her by the bandaged hand she decided to remove the bandage. She was hoping for a break from the endless questions from people she met. She was just a little tired of telling her story. It was a decision she was to regret. Following a few hearty handshakes on board the *Arakola* the wound re-opened and became infected. The ship's doctor eventually reduced the worst of the massive swelling when they docked in Calcutta.

Her aircraft was shipped by road to Calcutta's Dum Dum Airport and taken to the Indian Air Survey Company's workshops where it was carefully inspected. Their report was worse than she had expected. The aircraft was a 60 per cent write off. They estimated that it would cost £300 to repair. Not much less than the value of the aircraft. By today's standards £300 sounds a small sum. But when one realises that in 1979 a comparable light touring aircraft cost anything between $30 000 and $50 000, it is better understood how much £300 represented in 1933.

The manager of Indian Air Survey suggested that she had wasted money in bringing the wreck to India. His advice was to dispose of the remains, cut her losses and return home.

The repair problem involved not only the damage done

overturning in the surf. The wood and fabric airframe had also taken a terrible beating after all the manhandling, and successive loading and off loading that was necessary to get the plane as far as Calcutta. Thanks to her preventive maintenance, they could save the Gipsy engine; and the fuselage, wheels and spare propeller could be used again. But the rest, the delicate wings and tail plane surfaces, were little more than matchwood.

'This was a frightful blow and for a while I didn't know what to do. Three hundred pounds was a lot of money to pay to recondition her. But I just could not accept the fact that *My Little Ship* was finished. We had done so much together already that it seemed wrong not to finish this flight together. I was always reluctant to turn back without completing something I had started. At last, I told them to go ahead with the repairs. Once the decision was made I felt optimistic that everything would be all right.'

She was fortunate to meet an Australian couple, Mr and Mrs E. Payne, who insisted she be their guest during her wait in Calcutta. When she was not at the aircraft workshops checking on the progress of her repairs, she was taking in the sights of Calcutta. She was fascinated by the great beauty of the buildings, but taken aback at the hovels that the city's poor called home. People of obvious great wealth walked the street while in the gutters blind, legless beggars held out their bony palms. Women drew drinking water from the Hoogli River while the body of a dead child floated by, chased by a cloud of swooping vultures.

The three weeks of overhaul went slowly. For a while it seemed that an unobtainable mainspar would end her hopes. But one was found in Karachi and shipped by rail. Eventually all was reassembled. The only work left was the process of applying the protective dope to the wing fabric. Doping had the effect of shrinking the fabric drum tight and supplying a protective base for the paint. On the morning it was to be done, the rains came and the 'dry-weather only' process was put off.

To calm her frustration she took in more local sights.

She found she most enjoyed visiting the huge open market, where it was possible to buy anything from a pin to an elephant. She spent hours just 'window' shopping and taking in the kaleidoscope of noise and colour. The only thing that grated on her nerves was the habit the stall keepers had of flinging the change down on the counter instead of handing it to her. On one occasion, no longer able to contain her anger, she told a hapless proprietor, 'Pick that up and give it to me properly!'

The shopkeeper looked completely nonplussed, but did as he was told and she walked away with her nose in the air. When she recounted the episode to her hostess, Mrs Payne laughed and said, 'My dear, they do that deliberately. There are so many counterfeit coins in circulation. That is their way of telling whether or not the money is good. A counterfeit coin will not ring.'

The rain had passed and the doping was finished. The airworthiness inspector Jerry Randall arrived from the local office of the Department of Civil Aviation, to make a final check of the rebuild. He went over *My Little Ship* with a fine tooth comb. Three new wing sections, a new spar for the fourth, new tail section, a new spare propeller, new front cockpit cowling, and a new gravity fuel tank, and the remainder completely overhauled. He was satisfied with the workmanship and issued a new certificate of airworthiness. Company test pilot Graham Woollard took the Moth for its first flight and pronounced the aircraft as good as new. It was Mrs Bonney's turn.

She climbed aboard her aircraft and a few minutes later was over the outskirts of Calcutta. Once up she didn't want to come down again. The worry and frustration of the last month blew away with the slipstream. However, she noticed several minor adjustments were needed and that one of her blind flying instruments was not functioning, and landed quickly to get the work done.

Four more days went by before the instrument was fixed. On 5 May 1933, she finally left Calcutta bound for Allahabad. It had been five weeks since she had crash landed on Bang Biang Island.

7
Across Europe

As she had not been able to spend as long as usual running in her overhauled engine she decided to make several fairly short hops over the first few days. It is lucky she did. On reaching Allahabad, 700 kilometres inland, she found the whole lower side of the fuselage covered in oil. On checking the engine she discovered the auxiliary oil tank and the engine sump were almost empty. The auxiliary tank was split at the seam. Had she flown the 1100 kilometres straight through from Calcutta to Jhansi, as originally planned, she would have run out of oil in flight. That would have meant a seized engine and a forced landing.

The problem was overcome next morning when the auxiliary tank was isolated from the engine. The next leg of the journey, the 400-kilometre flight to Jhansi, went off without a hitch. But she noticed that visibility was deteriorating. Heat and dust haze made it almost impossible to pick out landmarks.

She refuelled and was off again bound for Jodhpur. She began to relax. The first few hours of flying after the massive overhaul were nerve wracking. It was quite common for mechanical problems to arise even after the very best service. And generally, pilots did not take off to cross a vast unknown continent until they had done enough flying to iron out the bugs. The oil 'bug' was ironed out and the Gipsy engine was running like a dream. All was well and England lay ahead over the nose. A long way admittedly, but she would get there now. She had been flying a 'dead-reckoning' compass course over flat featureless country for some hours. The visibility below was shocking. Suddenly she shook her head in disbelief. Something was terribly wrong. The sun, which should have been ahead to her left, was coming over her right shoulder. She had been so intent on steering an accurate compass heading she had somehow changed direction nearly 100 degrees. When had it happened? How long had she been heading in the wrong direction? And how had it happened? She found the answer to the last and vital question within moments. The verge ring of her compass had come loose and all the points of the compass and the 360 tiny markings, each representing one degree of direction, which were engraved on the ring, had flopped around. Another 'bug' to iron out, thought Mrs Bonney. Until it was realigned the compass was useless.

She could see a small settlement dimly through the haze. She decided to circle and try to work out a rough position. As she banked into a left turn she happened to glance directly below. To her astonishment she saw a large white circle on a field right under her wing. She knew that marking well. It was an aerodrome. She prepared for a landing.

A crowd swarmed around as she taxied to a stop. She asked the name of the village but they did not understand. Then she pointed at the village and said, 'Jodhpur?' They shook their heads and pointed in another direction.

'At this moment one of the villagers pushed his way through the crowd and informed me he was an English scholar. I asked him what the village was called. I was parched and asked for a drink of water. He produced a black umbrella of tent-like dimensions and shaded my way over to a small building. He stared at me all the time and finally asked, "What sex are you?" He must have been completely thrown by the flying suit and helmet. To say that I was taken aback is an understatement. But it was obvious from his intense look that he was genuinely puzzled. As soon as I could speak without spluttering I told him. He then asked, "What caste do you belong to?" This was too much, so I flippantly replied, "The lost tribes of Israel." He looked painfully confused so I eventually told him to forget it. I hurriedly got back into the aircraft and took off leaving him still trying to figure it all out.'

Now knowing the direction in which to head, Mrs Bonney roughly set the verge ring and picked up the railway line which led her right in to Jodhpur. Next morning a howling wind was blowing. With it came the thick dark sand storms that plague that part of the world in the dry season.

Aero Club instructor Goodwin was waiting at the club office. He advised her to wait a while for the storm to blow over. The previous evening he had shown her over two beautiful Monospar aircraft owned by the Rajah of Jodhpur. He suggested that they take a short flight in one which would give her some idea of flying conditions and visibility in the sand cloud. She thanked him but explained she had flown in similar and worse conditions over dust storms and bush fires back in Australia.

Half an hour later she was on her way to Karachi. Slowed down by head winds she crawled across the murky landscape. Near Hyderabad she had a terrifying experience. Swarms of large birds dropped down on either side of her aircraft. She avoided them by a fraction. Had they struck the aircraft she could have been in real trouble.

As she neared Karachi the ground became hilly and she encountered severe turbulence. On two occasions the bumps were so severe that the dirt and rubbish which had collected on her cockpit floor, flew up into her face. Thank heavens she had taken Captain Matheson's advice and equipped her aircraft with a full lap and shoulder harness. She was sure that if she had only had the more commonly used lap strap, she would have been thrown right out of the cockpit.

The 700 kilometres to Karachi took a tedious six hours. At the airport she found customs formalities even more tedious. It was petty officialdom at its worst with endless questions and a mountain of forms. Her bill of health clearance alone involved six different forms laboriously handwritten — in triplicate! There was no carbon paper. The aim of the exercise, it seemed, was to keep as many

Top: The Victoria Pensionat in Frankfurt, Germany, where the young Lores Rubens spent two years. *Bottom left*: Lores, aged sixteen, at the Victoria Pensionat. *Bottom right*: A portrait taken in 1917 for her wedding programme

Top: Mrs Bonney on her first flight with her cousin, Bert Hinkler. *Bottom: My Little Ship* immediately after it was purchased by Mrs Bonney's husband, Harry

Top: Mrs Bonney at Wangaratta after completing her first record flight. Her father, wearing the bowler hat, is standing by the cockpit. *Bottom*: Studying navigation theory for the flight around Australia

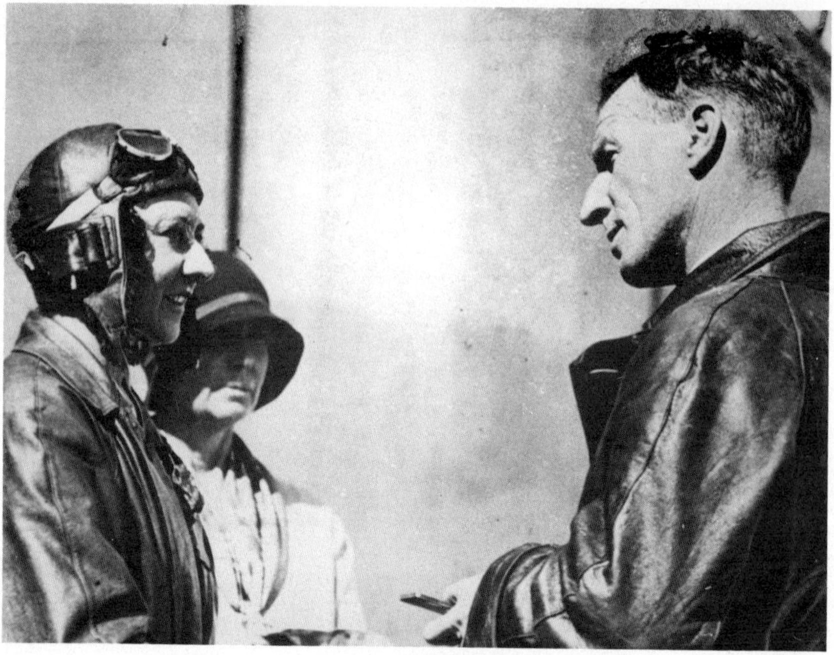

Top: 'You might make it if you've got the guts.' Discussing the round-Australia flight with Charles Kingsford Smith shortly before departure. *Bottom*: Mrs Bonney and an engineer inspect the engine of *My Little Ship* after the forced landing at Northfield, South Australia

Residents welcome the airwoman at the Wangaratta Town Hall on her round-Australia flight

Top: Minutes after this picture was taken over Victoria the Shell photographic aircraft collided with *My Little Ship* in mid air. No one was hurt. *Bottom*: Mrs Bonney was welcomed home after her round-Australia flight by her husband, Harry (left) and J.S. Mehan, the Shell Company representative

Top: The communal hut on Bang Biang Island where Mrs Bonney lived while awaiting rescue (Photograph by Lores Bonney). *Bottom*: District officer Khum and family alongside the wrecked Moth on Bang Biang Island (Photograph by Lores Bonney)

Top: Officers and mascot of the *Juna*. Captain le Britton is in the centre at the rear. *Bottom: My Little Ship* arrives at Dum Dum airport, Calcutta (Photograph by Lores Bonney)

Top: Mrs Bonney with the government test pilot, Graham Wollard, at Dum Dum. *Bottom*: Back in Brisbane after her Australia-England flight. The elegance of her Bowen Hills home fascinated the press

Mrs Bonney poses for photographers on her arrival at Croydon, England, after her third record-breaking flight

Top: Captain Ekrem Avni and his Turkish guards with Mrs Bonney and two friends at Adana. *Bottom*: Mrs Bonney and her Klemm 32, *My Little Ship* II, before (left) and during (right) her Australia-South Africa flight

Top: When Mrs Bonney landed in Cairo, the cabin of *My Little Ship* II was crammed with souvenirs collected along the route. *Bottom: My Little Ship* II aboard the flat-topped barge at Malakal, Sudan (Photograph by Lores Bonney)

Hair style of the Shilluk 'dandies' (Photograph by Lores Bonney)

Top: One of the paddle steamers which accompanied the Omurdman down the Nile to Khartoum (Photograph by Lores Bonney). *Bottom*: The RAF commanding officer and the three airmen who repaired the Klemm 32 at Khartourm

Top left: On safari with Captain Gethin (right) and Gethin's assistant. *Top right*: Mrs Bonney in 1955 about to place her metal pilot's wings on the Famous Flyers' wall at the St Francis Atrio Mission in California. *Bottom*: In 1981 Queensland schoolteacher Dorothy Dean recreated Lores Bonney's around-Australia flight, as a personal tribute to the pioneer. On completing the journey at Brisbane Airport, she was welcomed with a lei by her hero

In 1983, fifty years after the incident, Lores Bonney finally met the Qantas pilot who may have saved her life. Captain Russel Tapp was flying a Qantas mail run in 1933 in Camooweal, central Australia, while Mrs Bonney was on her flight to England. When it appeared Mrs Bonney was mistakenly heading into the Simpson Desert, Tapp chased the aircraft, and, using hand signals, eventually led her in the right direction (Photograph courtesy Queensland Newspapers)

officials as possible on the job. Six men to do a task that would be a breeze for one organised clerk.

The next day, while her aircraft was fitted with a new auxiliary oil tank, Mrs Bonney went looking for the permits she needed to cross Persia and Turkey. They had been pre-arranged by the Australian Department of Civil Aviation before she had begun her flight, and would be waiting on her arrival in Karachi.

She visited both consuls, but neither knew of her permits. They were most apologetic and promised to look into the matter immediately. It took ten days before they finally turned up. It was just as well she was not going for the speed record or she would have seen it slip away, sitting in a consulate while incompetent bureaucrats dithered around.

On 2 June the frustrated airwoman was on her way again. Stowed safely in her flying suit was a bundle of permits, visas, health certificates, general declarations, customs clearances, and even a personal letter of recommendation signed by the Persian consul. A great paper monument to small-minded bureaucracy. The airport health official required she carry triplicate copies of six different forms declaring her free of cholera, smallpox and yellow fever! However, even though reason told her the whole situation was like an Eastern farce, she did as he said. She knew she was likely to meet with more of the same bureaucratic nonsense before she reached London, and there was no way she was going to cool her heels for another ten days. It was also comforting to know that she still had most of the £500 travelling money she had started out with tucked away in her high lace-up flying boots. She was rapidly learning that in this part of the world petty government officials were not above asking for a small 'tip'. In some cases it was expected. Long-distance flyers crossing the Middle East, India and Asia always carried a large bundle of notes to 'grease the wheels'. The fuel and repair bills did not eat into her nest-egg. All her *en route* expenses were billed to her husband.

The day's flying took her first to Jask where she refuelled. There her papers were subjected to very close scrutiny by the poker-faced Persian authorities who finally waved her on. On the next leg to Bandar Abbas she was forced to fly through a thick sandstorm.

'I decided to carry on for as long as I could still see the coastline. It was a nasty experience. The sky and the desert formed a wall and the horizon was completely obliterated. I choked on the sand. Even the engine took on an odd and ominous note. The waters of the Gulf, roughened by the wind, turned muddy with churned up sand. The water was shallow and with no breakers it was difficult to pick out where the desert ended and the water began.'

The vicious desert wind cut her ground speed in half, and when she finally reached her destination 1170 kilometres later she had been in the air for nearly ten hours. She circled Bandar Abbas for several minutes looking for the landing ground. Nowhere could she see the tell-tale white circle or a windsock. She eventually picked the only piece of flat ground available, took the wind direction from a flag above an official looking building, and landed on the rough, pot-holed surface.

The tiny town with its mud-coloured, dome-shaped houses seemed deserted. But as soon as she climbed out of the cockpit, several cars turned up. Out of one emerged the inevitable customs official. He searched her and her aircraft thoroughly before signing her clearance. He looked disappointed.

There were no hotels, and one of the town's two European residents put her up for the night.

In the cool of the evening she decided to refuel *My Little Ship*. There was no funnel to fit into the tanks so the job was done transferring fuel from drums into small water jugs. Mrs Bonney was sitting astride the engine cowling when she noticed a helper arrive with a bedroom wash jug. He was waiting for it to be filled when a thought crossed her mind. She jumped down and inspected the new refueller's jug. There was a cup of water in the bottom. A minute or two later it would have joined the petrol in her tank. The result would have been disastrous.

It took three attempts to get off the ground next morning. Even at sunrise the temperature was approaching

30 degrees. By midday the desert temperature would exceed 40 degrees, and the sand would be too hot to walk on — even in shoes.

The 650 kilometres to Bushire were a nightmare. She had to contend with appalling head winds and sandstorms all the way, and, at one stage it took her three-and-a-half hours to cover 170 kilometres — an average speed of 48 km/h. She could have done better in city traffic, if she had learned to drive a car!

The British consul at Bushire informed Mrs Bonney that the winds would not drop till next morning, and on his advice the airwoman remained overnight as a guest of the Shell agent. Next morning she had more problems. The engine refused to start. More than likely it was a legacy from the previous day when the carburettor had sucked in the desert dust for several hours.

'I had lost a lot of valuable daylight working on her. In desperation I asked one of the officials to telephone the mechanic of the Air France mail plane that was due in later, on its way to Indo China. To my amazement the French mechanic sent a message that he did not consider it his job and was not prepared to give any assistance. I was dumbfounded. It was the first act of deliberate discourtesy among flying people I had encountered.'

The French aircraft came and went. Mrs Bonney was ignored by the crew and mechanic. As she watched their aircraft take off she was up to her armpits in oily engine and hopping mad!

After two hours of searching the maintenance manual, removing, cleaning and refitting parts, she again took hold of the propeller. She was almost too tired to swing it. She managed one mighty heave and the Gipsy burst into life.

The next leg of the journey was from Bushire to Basra and on to Baghdad. The head winds and sandstorms continued. The rough featureless desert and jagged mountain ranges seemed never ending, and the lack of detail on her Royal Automobile Club motor touring maps didn't help.

In 1933 proper aviation maps did not exist for most of

the world air routes and flyers did the best they could. The RAC had provided Mrs Bonney with her maps, but her cousin Bert Hinkler had navigated with a copy of *The Times* atlas on his epic 1928 flight.

After eight hours of sand, sweat, and bone-jarring turbulence the exhausted airwoman saw the tower-shaped minarets and blue-domed mosques of the ancient city of Baghdad.

For the first time since leaving Brisbane she was completely and utterly exhausted. Near collapse she was unable to answer the customs officer. An Imperial Airways engineer took control, pegged down her aircraft, and had Mrs Bonney whisked away to a nearby hotel. She was treated for heat exhaustion and made to dip her hands and wrists in bowls of iced water while ice packs were applied to the back of her neck. As her blood temperature dropped she improved rapidly. Later, she returned to the airport, completed formalities and arranged for a full aircraft service to be done by the expert Imperial Airways maintenance crew.

Accommodation, food, service, and all facilities in Baghdad were first class. However, there was one drawback to the paradise she had found in the middle of this inhospitable corner of the earth: sandflies. There were millions of them! She woke up in the middle of the night, itching all over and peppered with red spots. For a minute she was worried that she had contracted some skin disease, then with a dubious sense of relief she discovered the cause. Out came her mosquito coils and the problem was solved.

The next morning Mrs Bonney was embarrassed to find military guards lining her route to the airport. They really didn't have to go to all that trouble, she thought. It seemed too good to be true, and it was. The guard of honour was for King Faisal of Iraq who was also about to take off! However, she took off before the royal plane, leaving the King's pilot to taxi out through the clouds of her dust.

Between Baghdad and Adana, her first landing on Turkish soil, she encountered extremes of weather. The heat turned to a chilling cold and the sandstorms gave way to rain and later towering thunderstorms. She had hoped to make Konya by nightfall, but decided wisely to land at Adana. The last hour of the journey had been quite frightening with lightning forking on either side of her aircraft and well ahead she could see what could only be described as a huge barbed wire fence of glittering electrical discharge.

As she taxied in to the Adana airport she saw a group of soldiers waiting for her. She felt decidedly nervous. She had heard so many stories of hostile treatment meted out to European travellers in out of the way Turkish towns. Knowing no Turkish she had prepared a written list of what she hoped would be useful phrases, including 'Ben dama konusham osmani varde efendiler' ('I always understood the Turks to be gentlemen') and 'Bana zabitiya Getior' ('Fetch me a policeman').

Fortunately Mrs Bonney did not have to remind the Turks of their gallantry nor ask for a policeman. She was met by two charming army officers, Captains Ekrem Avni and Djmel Atram. Once the formalities had been attended to they placed a military guard on her aircraft and took her into town. At her hotel over cups of sweet Turkish coffee they checked her documents. What a pleasant change it made from some of her previous encounters with officialdom.

Next morning the helpful officers brought her the news that the weather was extremely bad. The bulletin advised her not to attempt leaving Adana, and promised further advice later. The two officers established themselves as her guides, hosts and bodyguards. They took her by taxi to Tarsus, the birthplace of Paul the Apostle, and later, since there was no petrol at Adana, they drove her to another town to pick up fuel for her aircraft. The whole journey was extremely arduous, with the taxi sustaining three punctures on the way, and by the time Mrs Bonney reached the petrol company office she was in no mood to be trifled with.

'I was already edgy after a taxi drive with three punctures. The driver had not been in the least concerned, and he carried no spare. Each time he had mended the tube painfully slowly. Anyway the final straw was when the petrol company official told me that they, the largest petrol company in the country, could not let me have any petrol.

'Is that really true?' I asked trying to remain calm.

'With the melancholy and unmoved politeness so typical of the country, and so infuriating at times, he replied, "Madam that is so." I stamped out of the room in a towering rage.'

She later regained her composure when a local family entertained her for tea in their beautiful garden.

When she climbed over the town next morning and set heading for Konya the Australian woman felt somewhat ashamed of the misgivings she had felt before her first contact with Turkish officialdom. The kindness and consideration she had been shown by her army hosts were quite overwhelming. She had not been able to solve the petrol problem but had checked her tanks carefully and worked out that there was enough to make the short hop to Konya. Maybe there she would be luckier.

She did find fuel at Konya but it cost a two hour delay, even though her army friends had telegraphed ahead. Nothing had been organised to get the fuel to the airport. When she was finally ready for takeoff, there was no wind, and to make matters worse the ground was so rough she had trouble getting the plane to accelerate to takeoff speed. Three-quarters of an hour and eight aborted attempts later she was ready to give up. But,remembering the Royal Automobile Club's warning not to stay overnight in primitive Konya, except in an emergency, she decided to try once more.

Picking the longest flattest run, she gave the engine full power from the start, brought the tail up as soon as possible, and adjusted the nose attitude for takeoff. Everything was set, but she was running out of flat land and was still not airborne. She was just preparing to throttle off and give it away, when the vibration of wheels on rough ground ceased. The tyres touched briefly on the turf one more time and then she was away.

She climbed slowly to 3500 metres for the seven-and-a-half hour flight to Constantinople across the mountains that covered the route as far as Eskisehir. Engine failure over this stretch would have meant certain death. There was nowhere to put an aircraft down in one piece. Mrs Bonney was rugged up in her cold-weather leathers again, but nevertheless she was numb with cold as she crossed the snow-covered ranges. She finally stopped shivering as she began a long slow descent to Constantinople.

That night she ate dinner outdoors overlooking the Bosporus. The setting had a dream-like quality. Thousands of tiny lights in the surrounding hills were reflected in the calm black water. It reminded her of the nights on Bang Biang Island and the fireflies. Had it only been six weeks before? At that moment it was hard to believe that the trauma of the island was not just a past nightmare.

The nightmare returned the next day, two hours after leaving Constantinople. Bound for Sofia, a little over an hour away she was flying high at 3500 metres to clear the mountains below, when threatening storms suddenly intensified and closed in around her. She turned quickly to head back to Plovdiv but it was too late. Another huge storm cloud had come up and now sat on the mountains barring her escape. She was trapped between layers of cloud, with storms forming a wall on all sides.

For five hours she circled around and around in the cloud-enclosed 'room'. There was nowhere to go. She would have no chance if she attempted to penetrate the black walls of rain, hail and turbulence-filled cumulonimbus. Far below were the deadly cloud-covered mountains and here and there she could see the peaks pushing up through the dull grey carpet of cloud. The white ceiling above was no escape either. It extended way above the limit that her aircraft could attain, and once in it, the airframe would pick up ice and the carburettor throat would slowly contract then close as the ice built up. When that happened the Gipsy engine would falter, then stop for good.

Even as she flew, more patches of cloud closed in

around her and at times she was forced to fly 'blind'. The hours under the blind flying hood at Archerfield were again paying off.

Things became even worse when her vital turn and balance indicator stopped working. She had great difficulty keeping the wings level in cloud. Turning became a chilling experience, and on one occasion she temporarily lost control and came diving out of cloud heading straight for the side of a mountain. She turned away just in time, but realised that the moment of reckoning had come. She would have to find a way down somehow. Her 'clear room' had finally disappeared. She was totally surrounded by cloud. She decided to follow the mountainside down.

'The ground at any price was my motto now. Feeling my way down carefully, almost at stalling point, several times I passed through clear patches and there would be a temporary easing of the strain. Then again, I would come into a dark patch, and turn away in fear that it might be the timbered side of the mountain showing through the cloud. It was a nightmare business, straining my eyes to penetrate the piled masses of opaque cloud, uncertain which might hide the danger of the mountain pressed in on either side. At last I came through a patch of filmy stuff, and with indescribable relief saw a railway line below.'

Thoroughly shaken Mrs Bonney followed the line to the first town, where she landed in a small paddock. She found a man who spoke French and managed to get directions to Plovdiv. She was lucky to be alive. Countless pilots in the same situation have been killed over the years and will no doubt continue to be so, as long as man remains fallible. Pushing on in bad weather for which neither aircraft nor pilot is sufficiently equipped is fatal and in Mrs Bonney's case the situation was worsened by the fact that not only did she not know the country but, she was also flying over mountains.

After reaching Plovdiv, she was delayed another day with fuel problems. Her flight to Sofia in clear weather took only ninety minutes.

She had been warned against taking the next leg of the journey by Ulm and Allan. The route included the Dragoman Pass. Nine kilometres wide with mountains on either side and prohibited airspace over the mountains, it was notorious for bad weather. Pilots avoided it like the plague if they had the choice.

She had decided to make London in one day. If she could manage the 2400 kilometres in one go she would establish a record. But she needed the right weather and winds. She got neither. Next day at 12.15 p.m. the weather finally improved sufficiently for her to fly to Budapest. She landed in time for tea, but was not allowed to leave the airport until four hours later. Officialdom had its way again. It was Sunday, and no one knew she was coming, so the customs officer was not on duty. Had it not been for the bad weather she would have pressed on to Vienna.

Recalling her problems with officialdom Mrs Bonney wrote in an article for the magazine *Table Talk* published later that year:

'To my mind there was entirely too much of the military and official element about such a flight as mine. I am still wondering how flyers set speed records. For me it was fatal to land, for immediately there would begin a third degree; very fatiguing to the nerves and temper!'

The problems Mrs Bonney found have not improved over the years, in fact with the splitting of the world into various camps it has worsened considerably.

Next morning she took off. She would make England non-stop. Everything was right. Poor Mrs Bonney. She had not counted on the ham sandwich she had eaten before takeoff. She was past Vienna and going well when she and the sandwich had a violent disagreement. She tried to carry on but she became increasingly worse. She had to get down quickly. She landed in a field, crawled out and started searching for her brandy flask. Within moments she was surrounded by local farming people. Feeling hemmed in, and violently ill she raced for the nearest house. The woman there gave her coffee and cognac, and when local police arrived, refused to let them in saying the airwoman was too ill. She was placed under guard while officials were sent for. Mrs Bonney had landed in the little town of Gmund, then a few hundred metres inside the Czechoslovakian border. The Czech officials were not impressed. Neither was the Australian airwoman. They were not interested that she had landed only because she had been taken ill. Conversation was carried out with the local station mistress acting as interpreter. She was a kindly soul and obviously embarrassed by the pig-headed attitude and rudeness of her countrymen.

A guard had been placed at her aircraft and she was not permitted to take off. The station mistress took her home and kept a friendly vigil until officials arrived from the nearby town of Budejovice.

For two hours she was questioned, her aircraft unpacked, everything examined and life made generally unpleasant. Finally, late in the afternoon, she was told she could leave. But it was too late and the field was not ideal for takeoff. She spent an unhappy night at the local hotel.

Next morning it was obvious she would not get off from the paddock. It was knee high in grass and soft from recent rain. She managed to obtain help to move the plane to a cart track. It was the best takeoff run available. Her first attempt failed. The track was too short and she ran off the end into the muddy ground of a young oat crop.

They pulled the aircraft out and were ready to try again when a large, furious woman, waving her arms and a wicked looking rake bore down on her. With blazing eyes and crimson face she stood screaming at Mrs Bonney. She shook her fist then pointed like a tragedy queen at the tiny area of damaged oats.

She seemed about to attack the stunned Australian when a police officer caught the irate woman by the arms. She broke free and stood centimetres away shaking her fists in front of the airwoman's face. Mrs Bonney eventually took cover behind her aircraft while the crowd watched doubled up in laughter at the whole farcical business. Eventually the police officer, trying his best to keep a straight face suggested that what she was after was financial compensation. He said she was demanding the equivalent of £10, which he added was outrageous. He suggested that the airwoman gave half of the amount. It did the trick.

She finally took off down the track with the men holding onto the wings of *My Little Ship*. Then opening up to full power she signalled them to release, and the little Moth lifted into the air. (This is similar to the short field takeoff technique employed by modern aircraft. Unlike the de Havilland 60, modern planes are equipped with brakes which do the job rather better than nervous hands on the wingtips.) Once airborne she took great delight in performing a mild but obvious beatup of the area.

She could only go as far as the Austrian town of Linz that day, a mere thirty minutes flying away. Before taking off from the unfriendly town of Gmund she had unloaded all her emergency supplies to lighten the aircraft for the difficult takeoff. The sympathetic station mistress had promised to put her kit on the next train to Linz. It was not due until the following morning.

The weather was good and she followed the River Danube. Conditions were perfect for once and she was tempted to carry on but realised she might never lay hands on her belongings again unless she arrived at the Linz station in person. Nevertheless, she stayed up for two hours overflying Linz into Germany. It was the most beautiful scenery she had ever seen. Eventually she backtracked and landed.

Unknown to Mrs Bonney, the telegram she had sent to Frankfurt while detained in Czechoslovakia, informing the authorities of her delay, never reached its destination. In fact, no official news of her had reached London since she had left Constantinople five days earlier. Communication was poor through the eastern European countries so it was not surprising that there was a growing concern for her whereabouts.

On 12 June the London papers carried the headlines, 'No News' and in Brisbane Harry Bonney was reported to say, 'While the absence of news is causing me some anxiety I am sure she has been delayed by some unforeseen occurrence. I am fully confident in her ability as a pilot and am sure she would take no risk.' In the same news item it was reported that Sir Charles Kingsford Smith had made an exhaustive study of her route. 'Mrs Bonney will probably be experiencing good weather. Conditions generally are most favourable for flying in Europe about this time of the year.' For once the famed airman was wrong. The foul weather that had plagued her from Turkey was to continue all the way to London.

It took her five more days to reach Frankfurt. She spent the first four at Linz. Her baggage had not turned up, and when it did, the weather had gone bad again.

Finally, on 17 June, she received a weather report that gave her a chance of getting through. She was airborne and within 200 kilometres of her destination when storms forced her to land at Wurtzburg-am-Main. There were groups of soldiers all over the airfield and she thought she was in trouble again. To her relief she found they were using the airfield for drill practice.

The weather did not clear till noon the following day and even then she was dodging storms all the way to Frankfurt. As she approached to land at the airport, which reminded her more of a small, well-manicured garden than a landing ground, Mrs Bonney sensed a restriction in her flying controls. Somehow the control column didn't feel it was moving freely. On landing she had it inspected but they could find nothing wrong.

While in Frankfurt she took a taxi to Homburg to revisit her old school. It was nineteen years since the tamed Australian rebel had been sent home from the cloistered halls of the Victoria Pensionat as a perfect young European lady.

It was a wet and miserable afternoon as she walked through the familiar streets to the Pensionat. She passed the restaurant where she and her classmates would stop for coffee during afternoon walks. At one corner she recalled an old man who sold them hot chestnuts from a burning brazier, and how she had held them in her pocket to warm her winter-chilled hands.

As she approached the school she longed to see her old

companions. She hoped that some of her old teachers would still be there, particularly those who had sweated over French and German lessons. She could tell them how invaluable the languages had been during the flight.

She was to be disappointed. Not only were all the old faces gone but the school had changed hands. It had been turned into a college for training young women in homecraft and business. Though bitterly disappointed she must have approved of the curriculum of the new school, particularly its emphasis on career training. She knew only too well the agonising boredom of highly intelligent women trained only for domesticity.

She revisited her old room and later, while walking in the grounds, she found the little patch of soil that had been her garden. She saw the huge pear tree which reminded her of the time when she and a friend had come within a hair's breadth of being caught stealing its fruit. They had perched breathlessly in its branches while her teacher stood below them. The penalty for offenders was severe, as a notice on the girls' bedroom walls had warned. But the notice had read 'If caught . . .' and that was the challenge for young Lores Rubens. It was the same sense of challenge that prompted her in later years to take on long distance flying records.

The following day it was still raining. She spent the morning cleaning her Moth and examining some local aircraft. She particularly admired a sleek low-winged Heinkel monoplane. Its streamlined fuselage and knife-thin wings were covered in varnished ply wood. Little did she realise that the beautiful machine was a forerunner of a fighter that was to equip Hitler's Luftwaffe. Built at a time when Germany was forbidden to produce weapons of war, the Heinkel was an aerial 'wolf in sheep's clothing', a carefully and cunningly executed exercise in fighter design.

After lunch the weather improved marginally. To obtain a better look she took on a joy flight a wide-eyed young boy who had begged her for a flight earlier in the day. Once up she thought she might get as far as Cologne and decided to push on after putting her passenger down.

The airport officials did not approve, but grudgingly conceded that with her experience she might get through. It took her just over two hours. She flew under low cloud and in rain all the way. But it was worth it — she was another 200 kilometres closer to London.

The flight almost ended early as she was turning in to her final landing approach at Cologne. The control column jammed as she eased it over to bank the aircraft. She was within seconds of the ground and had absolutely no control. Using both hands, she gave it an almighty jerk which freed it. Moments later she was safely down.

Following this nerve-wracking experience and remembering the feeling of restriction to her controls when approaching Frankfurt, she decided to have the aircraft's control system thoroughly checked. An engineer went over it in detail. Inspection plates were removed, control wires checked, aileron and elevator hinges scrutinised, bellcranks, control columns, the lot, were tested. Finally the puzzled man gave the Moth a clean bill of health. Rather disdainfully he suggested that it was probably a worn bolt leading to a little slackness which made it feel like it was jamming. 'Nothing to worry about,' he added.

Mrs Bonney was not at all satisfied with his offhand dismissal of the matter. She knew something was wrong and would not take off again until the mystery was solved. She insisted that the aircraft be checked again. The front cockpit had only been given a cursory inspection because its flying controls had been removed for the solo flight. She suggested that the engineer take a closer look. Showing obvious irritation at being directed around by this slip of a woman, he climbed up on the lower wing. He was muttering under his breath as he leaned into the cockpit, probably cursing the arrival of 'hysterical women pilots' into his world.

With Mrs Bonney's help he removed all the emergency equipment. This disclosed the protective canvas flaps covering the metal socket, in which the second control column would normally have been fitted for dual flying. With the flap open the mystery was solved. Wedged between the normally freely moving socket and its surrounds was a severely dented tin of bully beef, poised, ready to repeat its control freezing action.

Mrs Bonney was satisfied, and probably felt, a little smugly, that she'd made her point. The engineer departed, and it is hoped he paid more attention to the opinions of women pilots in the future.

It was too late to push on that day, which was frustrating as the weather had improved. The next day was a typical western European summer's day: it was raining! She waited until noon, and then with a slight improvement took off for England. All the way to the Belgian coast she was punching through rain and cloud. Most of the time it was blind flying on instruments. When she broke out near Bruges she was well off course. She headed for Ostend. From there it was a simple matter of following the coast to the regulation crossing point at Calais.

A huge storm lay over Calais. The hordes of deck chairs and gaily coloured umbrellas on the beach were deserted. Thirty-five kilometres over her right shoulder lay England; a quick hop across the channel. Rather than mix it with the storm she turned right early and headed out over the water. She was halfway across when the cloud broke, and there in glorious sunshine were the white cliffs of Dover. She made the crossing in fifteen ecstatic minutes.

As she headed for London she felt overwhelmed. She had made it. It didn't matter that she had not set a new speed record. That it had taken her ten weeks rather than twenty days was not important. She had set out to fly to England and she had done just that. And in doing so had become the first. Many women would follow her lead. Undoubtedly they would do it faster, but they could never be the first.

'As I flew from Dover to Croydon, I felt that the country I was travelling over was like the comfortable lap of some kind old lady. Perhaps it was because there were so many neat safe little fields below where I could have landed *My Little Ship* if necessary. Perhaps it was just the feeling of homecoming that even people of non-British parentage have told me they have experienced at first sight of England.'

Mrs Bonney was ten minutes ahead of her planned arrival time. For once the winds of Europe had been kind. As she approached Croydon to land she caught the slipstream of a huge four-engined Handley Page Hannibal airliner on the Imperial Airways run from Paris and was tossed all over the sky. Even a calm English summer evening could have its moments!

She taxied to the terminal area behind the huge biplane airliner and climbed out slowly from the cockpit. She was met by an airport official who was busy writing in a notebook.

'Where from?' he asked without looking up.

His head jerked back like a puppet in surprise when Mrs Bonney calmly replied, 'Australia.'

8
Apathetic Australia

Mrs Bonney had been in England only two weeks when she put the question to her husband Harry. Talking by phone to Brisbane she casually asked if he would mind if she flew home and had another go at the record. If she could find a faster aircraft in England she was sure she could break Amy Johnson's record.

'I would not like her to use the same aircraft again,' Harry Bonney told the press. 'But if she can find a new plane she certainly has my permission to fly back to Australia.'

Mrs Bonney got in touch with the de Havilland people in England and asked them if they could get her a new aircraft. It had to be able to cruise at least 30 km/h faster than her Moth and have equal or better range for her to be in the running for a new record.

She planned to leave in early October to pick up the best of the weather through India and the southern hemisphere. In the meantime what better oportunity than to see some of England by plane and get in a bit of flying.

The London press had made her an aviation celebrity, calling her 'Australia's own Amy'. Strangely enough the Australian press did not seem to pick up the catch phrase. Yet even the far off *Penang Gazette* used it when reporting that while in London she had written a 70 000 word book on the flight — in two weeks! That was something of a speed record, they remarked. Though never published in book form, her account of the flight was purchased by Melbourne's United Press and serialised in their weekly magazine *Table Talk*.

Shortly after arriving in England she presented her much travelled and autographed whisky bottle to the whisky manufacturer, Edward Young and Company. It was placed alongside C. W. A. Scott's record breaking bottle in the firm's London headquarters. Scott, a Qantas pilot, beat Kingsford Smith's England-Australia record in 1931 flying a DH Gypsy Moth.

On 8 July 1933, she was an honoured guest of the Royal Aero Club at the annual Kings Cup Air Races at de Havilland's Hatfield Aerodrome. Included in the forty-two entries was a DH Moth similar to *My Little Ship*. Mrs Bonney was pleased to see two women pilots among the competitors, Lady Bailey, an English devotee of sporting aviation and Mrs A. S. Butler. Both were flying de Havilland aircraft of the type the Australian woman hoped to obtain for her flight home. She watched spellbound with 100 000 others as a de Havilland aircraft took out the race. She also attended the RAF Annual Flying Display at Hendon, and flew to the north of England to enter *My Little Ship* in the Scarborough Aviation Display.

She did the normal tourist things too, visiting the Tower of London, Madame Tussaud's Waxworks, St Pauls, Westminster and the theatres. She was thrilled with London's West End and saw just about every show worth seeing.

But all the time she was planning, waiting for word on her new aircraft. De Havilland were building half of all aircraft produced in England. They were also the world's major supplier of light aircraft. In the early 'thirties the American aviation industry had not yet started to compete in the light aircraft field. De Havilland aircraft were in demand everywhere, especially the new 200 km/h Puss Moth. The latter, Mrs Bonney thought, would be ideal for her return trip with its high wing and enclosed cabin. The problem was how to obtain one.

A letter from her father ended her dream. He had been in poor health, and though he was much recovered since hearing she was safe after her Bang Biang episode, he felt his health could not stand the anxiety of a return flight.

She was bitterly disappointed and also worried about the news of her father's illness. She immediately booked passage home on the Orient Line steamer RMS *Otranto.* She sailed from Tilbury Docks on 2 September 1933. The London *Daily Sketch* recorded her departure with the headline, 'If only she could fly back home.'

'My only regret is that I am not flying home,' she told the reporter. 'I have no regrets about the flight here. Though I was dogged with bad luck, I did the journey. I feel sure I could break the record if I were flying home.'

When the *Otranto* docked in Melbourne six weeks later, *My Little Ship* was safely tucked in a packing case in the liner's hold. Australian papers were already reporting her intention to make another record attempt. But for the moment Mrs Bonney decided that must wait. It was high time to revert to Mrs Bonney — homemaker.

After visiting her father she returned to Brisbane and soon settled back into life at Jordan Terrace. In six months Brisbane had not changed. There were a few new faces at the Aero Club. She was occasionally in demand as a guest speaker, invariably at women's meetings, but it was not long before the flight became a distant memory.

Early in December her aircraft was back at Archerfield and ready to fly. She did a quick test flight and a few days later flew down to Wangaratta to see her father. The eleven-hour flight seemed child's play after her England adventure.

Since her arrival back in Brisbane in mid-October, articles and letters had regularly appeared deploring the lack of public interest and formal recognition of her flight.

The *Telegraph* front page headline on 3 November, two weeks after she arrived back, read 'No honour in her own Country'. It went on to accuse Brisbanites, especially women, of complete apathy. It remarked how thousands had greeted Amy Johnson yet only a handful of friends were at Archerfield to greet Mrs Bonney. The *Courier Mail* joined the fray in deploring the lack of recognition in her own town. It, too, singled out the city's women for special criticism.

Soon the general public were involved and letters to the editor were carrying the observations of the man and woman in the street. Invariably they said the same thing. What a poor show by Brisbane, particularly its women!

Some of the leading lights of the city's women's organisations went to press in defence. 'Ours is a business league not really involved in social matters,' said one pompously. The National Council of Women suggested, 'If she had come the other way, instead of finishing in England and then coming home by boat, the excitement would not have died down.' The Town and Country Women's Club stated, 'It had been intended to honour her on her arrival but owing to pressure of business matters the club was prevented from achieving its desires.'

Whichever way you look at it they were not really interested. Apathetic Queensland! And what of the men. Nobody thought of criticising them specifically. Well Mrs Bonney was a woman wasn't she? If it had been a man setting some sort of record it would have been a different matter!

Mrs Bonney remained apart from the bally-hoo. She had made the flight as a personal challenge. She was smart enough not to be surprised at Brisbane's public reaction. It is more than likely that most Queensland women, tied to husband, home and children, resented her freedom and the notoriety it had brought her. In an era where women's place was firmly established in the home, most would have believed it to be Mrs Bonney's place also. If the truth were really known, they were probably jealous of her seemingly glamorous lifestyle.

When recognition finally came, it was from England. King George V awarded her the M.B.E. in the June 1934 Birthday Honours List, in recognition of the pluck, perseverance and skill of a pioneer among Australian airwomen.

Throughout 1934 Lores Bonney used *My Little Ship* to help promote an interest in aviation among the young, taking groups of children on their first flights. And in June of that same year *My Little Ship* was one of the formation of Royal Queensland Aero Club aircraft that escorted the New Zealander Jean Batten and her black kitten mascot into Archerfield. The civic reception held in Miss Batten's honour sparked off the criticism that no official welcome had been given Brisbane's own aviatrix.

News came from overseas that Americans had recognised her achievement. Mrs Bonney, along with England's Amy Johnson, was made a governor of the Women's International Association of Aeronautics.

Throughout 1935 she was secretly planning another attempt at the England–Australia record. Always on the lookout for a more suitable aircraft, she was given the opportunity of flying a Germen-built Klemm Eagle monoplane. Like her Moth, the sleek cabin aircraft was powered by a Gipsy engine and it was 30 km/h faster than her biplane. Though still the backbone of the aero club movement de Havilland biplanes were becoming outdated for record breaking and aerial touring. The superior speed, range and comfort of cabin monoplanes were attracting the record breakers. Jean Batten had changed to a Percival Gull monoplane and Amy Johnson had given up her Moth *Jason* in favour of the high-wing, cabined Puss Moth. Mrs Bonney was smitten with the Klemm and decided that when one became available she would make the change.

In mid-1935 she made a 6500 kilometre flight around northern and central Australia, taking in Cairns, the Gulf of Carpentaria, Mount Isa, Alice Springs and a meandering route across outback Queensland on the return flight. Though publicly on holiday and visiting the Aboriginal missions, she was also keeping her hand in, working on navigation over the vast and desolate inland country. She already had another flight in mind.

She had entered a number of small air races over the years, with mixed success. So it was natural that when the South Australian Government announced their intention of holding an air race as part of the State's centenary celebrations, Mrs Bonney decided to enter. It would give her a chance to try out her latest acquisition — the Klemm 32 *My Little Ship* II.

Her husband had bought it a month earlier from a

Brisbane pilot, N. B. Littlejohn, who had recently flown the monoplane out from England with his bride. Mrs Bonney had felt the pang of losing an old friend when her little Moth was sold, but soon got over it in the excitement of converting to the new and more sophisticated aircraft.

She almost came to grief on one of her first flights when the engine cut dead over Brisbane. The only clear landing area was a nearby golf course. With insufficient altitude she could not quite reach the fairway. Like an ill-directed golf ball she landed in the rough! Golfing fanatic Harry Bonney would have been appalled with such a 'lie'. As the Klemm bumped to a stop the undercarriage caught in small shrubs, slewed the aircraft around, and one leg collapsed. It was quickly repaired for the race. Freda Thompson, Australia's first woman flying instructor, entered a Gipsy Moth; May Bradford, a charter pilot from Mascot, was flying a Klemm Eagle; Nancy Bird, another commercial pilot, was in command of a Leopard Moth; and Ivy Pearce, a member of the Royal Queensland Aero Club, who specialised in aerobatics, piloted a twin-engined Monospar, with her future husband, Jason Hassard.

The race got under way on 16 December 1936. The 2300-kilometre route included overnight stops at Sydney and Melbourne. Thirty-one aircraft took off from Archerfield at three-minute intervals. Slowest first and fastest last. Mrs Bonney's Klemm, one of the speedier aircraft, was number twenty-one on the starting line. 'Scratch' pilot, J. W. Collins of Queensland, was the last to go in his 200 km/h Percival Vega Gull.

H. F. Broadbent, holder of round-Australia and England-Australia speed records, was a hot favourite. Queensland commercial pilot P. H. Moody in his American Stinson Reliant had the second fastest aircraft and was considered by many as Queensland's best hope.

Strong tail winds assisted most competitors on the first leg and Broadbent's DH Tiger Moth was first across the line at Mascot, though on handicap he slipped to seventh place. Fastest time for the day went to Collins closely followed by Moody. Mrs Bonney, who at times had attained a ground speed of 250 km/h was, like the other fast aircraft, well down the list when the handicaps were applied. The strong tail winds had favoured the slower aircraft, with the handicapping system used. Those flying fast machines were praying for head winds next day.

It was a disastrous day for four flyers. They caught the worst of the storms that built up along the course later in the day. The reporter for Brisbane's *Courier Mail*, who followed the race in Captain P. G. Taylor's Percival Gull, wrote:

'The section from Cootamundra onwards, with its mountain and forest almost claimed at least one victim, and three pilots were forced down by a huge storm that swept in from the east.

'The "Flying Fiddler" [P. Moore McMahon] who is said to be carrying his £2000 violin with him, came down 25 miles south of Benalla, and was so badly bogged that he was unable to reach Essendon. He hopes to join the race tomorrow.

'P. Mulholland made a forced landing outside Sydney, and did not come on.

'Mrs Bonney and H. Plumridge were both forced down by the heavy storm and lost much time. Mrs Bonney heroine of many long flights lost so much time trying to avoid the storm that she grew anxious about her petrol supply. The weather was "too dirty" to go on she said. She circled over Bangalore Station several times and saw Bond's Moth on the ground, he having been forced to land. This decided her to land also and she came down at Seymour at 4.30 p.m.'

Mrs Bonney, unlucky again with weather, was now well out of the running. When she finally reached Essendon, the delay had cost her three hours. Late next day when the aircraft had reached Adelaide and the handicaps were worked out, a little-known pilot flying his Porterfield had won the great race. His name was Reginald Ansett.

The race had been a disaster for Mrs Bonney in terms of positional performance. But the air race had given her a golden opportunity to critically evaluate the Klemm's performance for a much more important flight she had in mind.

Shortly after returning to Brisbane she was involved in a moment of Australian aviation history that was to make the name of an unknown Queensland bushman, Bernard O'Reilly, a household word.

The Airlines of Australia tri-motored Stinson airliner took off from Archerfield on 19 February 1937. It was bound for Sydney. Forty minutes later it disappeared without trace. A massive air search was launched. RAAF, commercial and private aircraft took part in the hunt. For seven days forty aircraft scoured the Stinson's route. Mrs Bonney joined the search, basing her aircraft at Grafton. Jean Batten also took part in her new Percival Gull.

In three days Mrs Bonney made five long search flights. On the second day she was airborne for nearly eight hours flying in turbulent conditions over the wind-swept coastal ranges, but like the others saw nothing.

The search continued until a grieving nation heard that bushman O'Reilly had set off alone, on foot, through the dense mountain bush of the McPherson Range and had found the wreck. He had played a hunch that the search was being conducted in the wrong area and had worked out where he felt the downed aircraft would be. Alongside the burned out wreckage he had found two survivors. Five others, including Captain Rex Boyden, had died in the crash. Their deaths were overshadowed by the news of O'Reilly's gallant and intuitive two-day trek. A grateful Australia rejoiced and Bernard O'Reilly earned a lasting place in aviation history.

The month following the Stinson crash, Brisbane newspapers carried another lead aviation story. Mrs Bonney was planning to fly from Australia to South Africa. If she made it she would become the first pilot, man or woman, to link the two nations.

9
No Place for a Woman

It was Harry Bonney who first suggested the South Africa flight to Lores Bonney. He knew that since her 1933 England trip she had been pining for another record attempt. But she had been thinking in terms of the speed record between the two countries. His suggestion changed her whole line of thinking. Like her earlier flights speed would not be essential for the Australia-South Africa flight. If she could reach Cape Town she would be the first, and not just the first woman. That appealed to her. Like most pioneer airwomen she was tired of flying behind and in the shadow of men.

It was with this flight in mind that her husband had purchased the Klemm. From the early days of anxious acceptance of her flights, his attitude had blossomed into enthusiastic encouragement. In recognition of this fact she publicly flew under the name of Mrs Harry Bonney. Only to her closest friends was she Dolores, or Lores as she preferred.

She was also painfully aware that she and her husband had not had children. Raised in the belief that marriage and children were synonymous, she was deeply concerned for her husband's feelings knowing that there would be no children to carry on the family name. She felt that if her flights were done in his name and perhaps one day recorded in Australia's aviation history, then she would have repaid his kindness in some small measure and kept the Bonney name alive.

South Africa, that would be a flight to be remembered! There was also a spin-off for her. It was the country of her birth and she had always hoped to go back one day.

Cape Town had become the fashionable destination for the long-distance record breakers from England in the 'thirties. The Australia–England record had been done over and over. The adventurers looked for somewhere new to catch the imagination of the public. Where better than across the Sahara Desert and the savage jungles of Africa, where one mistake or plain bad luck meant agonising death by thirst in the Sahara, or a mercifully quick end beneath some jungle canopy. Africa appealed to the ghoul that lurks in every sporting spectator.

Though the South Africa flight was not to involve her in the high drama that had accompanied the England trip, nor win her the same press coverage, there is no doubt whatsoever that it was the most significant of Mrs Bonney's flights. It was by far the most difficult. Few non-professional pilots, even with today's modern aircraft, would undertake the flight in a single-engined aircraft. In 1937 it was an incredible undertaking. Just under 30 000 kilometres, and most of it over savage wilderness.

She considered the time element for the flight in great detail. If she were to average eight hours flying per day at an average cruising speed of 160 km/h the flight would take a month. This estimate was quite generous, allowing for the vagaries of the winds which seemed always on the nose and a few days on the ground for servicing *en route*. However, she knew from bitter experience that shortage of aircraft facilities along her little travelled route, and the delaying problems of bureaucratic red tape, could add considerably to that time. She decided to make no attempt at setting a breakneck speed for the flight. Since she would be the first she decided to be satisfied with that knowlege and take a little time to see more than just hotel rooms along the way. She would set her own pace as the situation dictated. She allowed two months.

The flight was to her mind an ideal opportunity to benefit her country in some way and she approached the Australian Government. She had been made aware of the importance of tinned foods during her England flight. In the underdeveloped tropical regions of the world, where refrigeration was unknown, or rather the prerogative of the rich, canned foods were the only alternative to local foodstuffs. Fresh food was virtually non-existent in many of the barren areas she would visit. She suggested that she might organise the promotion of Australian tinned foods at such places along her route.

To her surprise the government was not interested. Prime Minister Lyons did, however, send a letter of goodwill from the people of Australia for her to carry on the flight. It was addressed to the people of the 'other lands' she was to visit.

On 9 April 1937, one day short of four years after her England flight, Mrs Bonney took off for Cape Town. Quite a crowd had gathered around her blue and silver Klemm. The press were out in force and she was also interviewed by the newsreels and radio.

She had recruited Qantas chief engineer Baird and his men to prepare her aircraft for the flight. The friendship and respect that went back to her 'apprentice' days had not wavered. Her first instructor, Charles Matheson, was again there to see her off.

With a minimum of fuss she kissed 'hubs', climbed on board and shortly after 8 a.m. she was in the air.

'We all know the aeroplane is not the master of the elements,' Harry Bonney said after she had taken off, 'and my definite instruction to her is that she must not fly in bad weather. She has promised to wait for favourable conditions at all times.

'Having flown with my wife on many trips I have not the slightest doubt that, given reasonable weather, she will accomplish her trip successfully,' he added before returning to his office.

However, it was obvious Mrs Bonney's idea of favourable conditions and those of her non-flying husband varied considerably, otherwise it is doubtful if she would have ever reached Cape Town.

Her first day's flying would take her as far as Blackall. Once on her way, she had time to relax and reflect a little on the last hectic days of preparation. She recalled with pleasure the letters she had received from total strangers asking to be carried as paying passengers on the flight. She appreciated the confidence they had shown in her; however, she felt bitter towards organisations which early on in the piece had jumped at the chance to sponsor her but had later backed down when asked to honour their promises. Apparently, 'they were so concerned with the loss of so many leading airmen that they felt it would be in Mrs Bonney's interests if they withdrew their backing.'

She also mentally ticked off her equipment and luggage to make sure that nothing was left out that she might need later. As on her first flight overseas, she carried a carefully planned emergency kit. Her personal baggage included a slightly bigger wardrobe than last time. One of the advantages of not going all out for speed was that she would have time to get out of oily overalls during her stopovers. Being an airwoman was no excuse for not being properly turned out when the occasion dictated!

The flight to Blackall took her seven-and-a-half hours. The weather was perfect and with light winds from the south-east she averaged 172 km/h. On arrival Blackall airport appeared rather small, so she elected to land behind the racecourse. After tying down her aircraft and organising for someone to keep an eye on it through the night, Mrs Bonney rushed into the town to buy a watch. She had been confused with her navigation that day when she had noticed a large variation between her aircraft clock and her two wrist watches. For a while she was unsure of the exact time.

Next morning she was at her aircraft early. She planned to make Brunette Downs that day, but was shattered to find a hole the size of a fist in the tailplane during her pre-flight inspection. Vandals had neatly sawn a piece out of its plywood covering. This sort of senseless souveniring was not uncommon. Mrs Bonney dug out her emergency kit and patched the hole, while the local Shell representative took the opportunity to fix the aircraft's erring clock.

Due to this delay she only reached Camooweal on the second day. The flight had not been without its problems. To conserve space and avoid folding and unfolding her maps, she had prepared them in strips and strung them on rollers. As she moved across country she was able to move the map along to correspond with the area she was flying over. Unfortunately, during the flight the maps came off the spools and she had great difficulty handling the long narrow strips in the confined cockpit.

The following day she made Darwin in six-and-three-quarter hours flying non-stop. Conditions were perfect. It was so smooth that she was able to write a letter to her husband during the flight. She housed her aircraft for the night in the Qantas hangar alongside a huge German Junkers cargo plane and the Qantas aircraft bound for Singapore the next day.

The following day she had *My Little Ship* II thoroughly serviced for the gruelling Timor Sea crossing. Since leaving Brisbane she had been experiencing carburettor problems. The engine had been intermittently running too rich. She spent all day with the mechanics going over the aircraft and after a one-hour test flight late that afternoon, *My Little Ship* II was ready. The little plane carried seven hours' fuel for the estimated five-hour overwater flight, and a fully-equipped inflatable life raft was on board just in case.

Before she left on 13 April she told a waiting journalist, 'I am not superstitious and have no qualms about crossing the Timor on the 13th. The only good luck charm I carry is a small compass which was on my father's watch fob. It has been made into a wrist band.'

Mrs Bonney had no time for the fashionable vogue of carrying all sorts of good luck charms to keep away the 'gremlins'.

She took off from the Ross Smith aerodrome at 6.45 a.m. and landed at Kupang four-and-a-half hours later. For the second time she had a following wind and other than striking smoke haze from bushfires on the Australian coast, she had an uneventful crossing. Her average speed had been 192 km/h.

The next day she got a terrific shock. After landing at the island of Lombok, a group of native soldiers advanced on her aircraft with poised spears. What had she done wrong now? Captain Johnson, the director of the Department of Civil Aviation had advised her that approval had been granted from all authorities along her route to South Africa. Yet there she was being menaced only a day out from Darwin!

She sighed with relief when the troops lowered their wicked looking weapons, smiled and turned around. They were practising a welcoming ceremony for the governor of Batavia. She hoped he would be better prepared than she was.

After leaving Lombok she met the inter-tropical front near Bali. The good weather had gone, and with a vengeance. Unable to distinguish between the wall of black rain and the mountains she was forced to turn back to Lombok.

She tried again later in the day, but got caught in heavy rain within a few kilometres. With visibility down to a few metres and no horizon she was forced onto instruments. She breathed a word of thanks to her friend, Freda Thompson, the Victorian instructor, who had offered her the use of her new Sperry Artificial Horizon for the flight. The instrument, a vast improvement on the old turn-and-bank indicator, gave an accurate picture of the aircraft's attitude in relation to the horizon. Though still demanding undivided attention it made the lot of a trained instrument pilot considerably less nerve wracking.

Mrs Bonney fixed her attention on the tiny aeroplane in the instrument's centre, and with occasional cross checking of her other instruments, pushed on through the 'soup'.

When she reached Surabaya three hours later the airport was bathed in sunshine. Local officials suggested that she had picked a bad time of the year to make the flight through the area. It was, they told her, the change-over of the seasons. She explained that she had to consider the weather all the way to South Africa and reach a compromise.

That night in the local hotel the airwoman tucked into a good meal. But she was not going to get caught again. Remembering the previous food poisoning episode on the last flight she chose very carefully from the menu. She was not going to drink local water or eat fresh fruit, salads, fish, or uncooked foods of any description.

The engine required minor servicing at Surabaya, so she was not ready until 10 a.m. on 16 April. Heavy clouds still hung around but the local pilot thought she would get through. She covered the 650 kilometres to Batavia in a little under five hours. Cruising low below the cloud gave her a chance to see the brilliant green vegetation of the islands and the clear waters around them. Now and again she caught fleeting glimpses of native villages and tiny people in bright-coloured batik staring up and waving as she passed overhead.

The calm beauty on the ground contrasted sharply with the ominous black storm clouds building up over the islands far ahead. But they seemed past her destination. There would be time enough to worry about them the next day. With any luck they would clear overnight.

She determined to make a very early start. It didn't help. When she studied the weather to the west next morning, the sky was as black as ink. It had rained all night. Her memories of Batavia as a beautiful spot had been ruined. This time it was all dripping trees, mud, and depressed-looking people.

Three hours later the sky seemed brighter and the rain had gone. She headed for Singapore 1000 kilometres away. She was half way there when she hit a solid wall of storms near Muntok. It was impossible to get through. Remembering her disastrous episode at Bang Biang four years earlier she was determined not to get caught again. She turned around and headed back the 30 kilometres towards Banka Island which she knew had an emergency landing ground. But already storms were breaking in that direction. She was forced to circle for two hours. Five times she attempted to find a way through the barricade of rain storms and each time she was forced back. Her aircraft was being tossed around in extreme turbulence.

Then suddenly her faithful Gipsy engine, which had never missed a beat, started to run 'rough', making it vital that she land immediately. Even the Klemm's beautifully constructed and tightly fitted engine cowling could only take so much. Moisture had entered the engine compartment and was obviously affecting the magnetos and spark plugs. Every minute it was getting rougher. She must land.

She searched through the rain streaked windscreen for the landing ground. Luckily she was close to Banka when the engine lost power. She saw that the channel between the island and Sumatra was whipped with huge waves. The wind was getting worse. The rain came in again but not before she caught a quick glimpse of the cleared area. She raced the wall of rain and just beat the worst of it, landing safely. On arrival Mrs Bonney got slowly out of the cabin. She was physically and emotionally exhausted. She had been in the air only six hours but it felt more like sixty.

She went straight to the post office and sent a telegram to the RAF in Singapore telling them she was down safely. That night she was a guest of the only European family on the tiny island. On the same evening, while she was lingering over her after-dinner coffee, she heard the news from Singapore come over the radio.

'Grave fears are held for the safety of Mrs Bonney. She is reported three hours overdue on a flight from Batavia. The RAF have asked shipping in the area to be on the lookout for her aircraft.'

Mrs Bonney was understandably furious. Several hours had passed since she had lodged the cable, yet it obviously had not reached Singapore. With her luck, she thought, United Press would already be flashing the news to Australia and everyone would be worried for nothing when they opened the papers next day. Her hosts rushed her to the post office in their car, only to discover that the message had just gone off. The sleepy islander in charge had not thought there was any hurry!

The weather did not improve during the night so she spent the next day exploring the island. She couldn't resist buying a few tiny pieces of jade and lapis lazuli jewellery from a Chinese merchant. She could find a spot for them somewhere and they weighed next to nothing.

A break in the weather came on 19 April and she made Singapore in three-and-a-half hours. Her total flight time at that stage was a shade over thirty-one hours; nineteen hours less than it had taken in her Moth *My Little Ship*. It passed through her mind that the Klemm could possibly beat the latest England to Australia record set by Jean Batten in her Percival Gull.

While in Singapore Mrs Bonney learned that a cholera epidemic had struck Bangkok and that hundreds were dying every week. She had planned to pass through that city, but if she carried on it was likely she would be quarantined and inoculated. She knew that the effects of inoculation would delay her there for some time. The alternative was to follow the east coast to Rangoon and avoid Bangkok altogether.

It took all afternoon and much of the next morning to get the necessary maps and approval from the controller of Aviation. She made Penang late in the afternoon and booked in to the Runnymeade Hotel at Georgetown. Taking in the view of the bay she understood why the island had become the favourite holiday spot of the thousands of colonial Europeans throughout Indo-China. It lived up to its title of 'Pearl of the Orient'.

A mishap while landing at Alor Star, just 100 kilometres north of Penang was a blessing in disguise. She was landing to take on maximum fuel for the flight to Tavoy, when the tyre of her starboard wheel blew, and *My Little Ship* II groundlooped, but fortunately remained undamaged.

The blown tyre was not fixed till late that day and she was forced to stay at Alor Star overnight. The next morning while she was waiting at the airport for a satisfactory weather report, she received a message from the Imperial Airways pilot who had just flown her intended route. He warned her not to use the West Coast under any circumstances. Terrific storms were all over the area and would last three or four days.

As it was on this leg of her England flight that Mrs Bonney had come to grief, she needed no further warning. She again revised her flight plan and headed for cholera-stricken Bangkok. It was the lesser of the two evils.

There was a second and more recent reason for not mixing with the weather up the coast. When reported overdue at Singapore, Mrs Bonney had come in for some rough treatment from the *Singapore Free Press*. The paper had suggested that the local authorities were getting tired of solo stunt pilots and their antics. Believing her to be lost, when in fact she was safe on Banka, an obviously unairminded journalist had criticised her for the unnecessary cost of an impending land, sea and air search. He referred to her forced landing at Bang Biang and the enormous expense of the massive search launched on that occasion. It seems he had not taken the trouble to research the matter very deeply or he would have found the 'massive search' had involved one RAF flying boat, normal shipping on the lookout, and a 30-kilometre trek by an islander who had been paid with Mrs Bonney's watch. Once located she was, admittedly, visited by the district officer, Khum, and his family and rescued by the two tin miners, but the Singapore authorities were not charged for their assistance.

The article concluded by suggesting that any pilots who wished to make such hazardous flights in single-engined aircraft should lodge a sum of money sufficient to defray the costs of a search with all authorities *en route*.

One must be grateful that the governments of the world took no notice of this rather liverish journalist. Had they decided to ban flights without the deposit of the huge sums required to search, it would have been a sad day for aviation. The record breakers and route pioneers of the 'twenties and 'thirties were invariably flying on a shoe string budget. Such an impractical imposition would have strangled aviation in early childhood.

The lone flights of the early pioneers were the launching pads of commercial aviation and the early faltering steps of the international airlines. Bleriot, the Smith brothers, Hinkler, Lindbergh, Kingsford Smith turned the eyes of the world upwards and after them came the slowly growing band of record chasers, opening routes between nations hitherto unlinked by air. Their quest for speed and distance brought constant and radical improvements in aircraft design and performance, all of which was to eventually benefit the airborne passenger. Had they not done so, the growth of the aviation industry would have crept along at a snail's pace.

For poor Mrs Bonney, who had been singled out for such abuse, the problem was not to try and convince a pompous journalist of the importance of long distance flying, but to pass through safely to Bangkok. Thus she would disprove his theory that she would probably have to be 'snatched from the jaws of death' by a rescue team in some 'inaccessible spot'.

She reached the Thai capital in the middle of the afternoon. In 1937 Bangkok was renowned as a city of temples and the centre of the old nation of Siam. From the air she had seen the sunlight flashing from its famed temple tiles, and the mass of scarlet and green and blue and gold had reminded her of a distant bed of blooming flowers.

The welcome she received at Bangkok was heartening after her rather miserable departure from Singapore. The Union Jack was flying in her honour as she landed at the airport and a formation of military aircraft also gave a display of aerobatics as a courteous gesture to her arrival. The Bangkok press, too, were delighted with her visit. They were, however, disappointed that she gave no interviews. This was understandable after her encounter with the Singapore press but, in fact, she had also promised exclusive rights to her story to a group of Australian newspapers. Nevertheless she posed for cameramen and later that night went on radio.

She was delayed in Bangkok by bad weather. Three times she attempted to take off for Tavoy, and each time she was forced back by the monsoon storms. The Imperial Airways pilots had been quite right; no way could she cut back across to the west coast.

She had taken the precaution of being inoculated at Alor Star and so she was able to take in the sights of the epidemic-ridden city. She noticed the contrast between the beauty of the 300 temples and the filthy poverty of the swarms of boat people who lived in the backwaters of the canal. When she saw the way in which meat, fish and fruit were displayed in the open markets, where they were covered with dirt and swarming flies, it was easy for her to understand how disease could spread like wildfire through the city.

With its Siamese fighting fish, sacred white elephants, temples, bazaars and canals, the city contained many diversions that helped to fill the days of waiting. One custom particularly intrigued her. She noticed that seed pearls seemed very popular and sold well at the bazaar stalls. She watched the locals carefully selecting their purchases, but stood in utter disbelief as she saw them pop the pearls into their gaping mouths and swallow them. What a waste of her favourite jewel she thought when told they were being taken for medicinal purposes.

After a week in Bangkok, Mrs Bonney was restless, but the weather was still bad. She talked with a British airline pilot who had just pushed through from Rangoon. He told her that nobody knew just how high the mountains were, and that with the weather as it was, it would be madness to carry on.

'No place for a woman,' he added. 'Best thing you can do is pack up and go home.'

That did it. She would get through somehow.

There was a slight improvement on 1 May. Against all advice she decided to try and reach Tavoy, only two hours away. If conditions became worse she would return. Constantly on her guard, and making sure that her escape route back remained clear she edged her way across the peninsula. Before the afternoon storms broke she was on the ground at Tavoy.

That night her host, an Englishman working for the Public Works Department, told her an intriguing story.

Just eighteen months earlier the Englishman's native house boy had been talking with a friend at the local market. The 'friend' had just returned from a fishing trip around the islands off the Burmese coast. One night the fishermen had heard a noise and then seen a big light in the sky go down into the sea some distance off. They had no idea what it could have been. It was some weeks later when the story got back to the house boy's employer. Knowing that Sir Charles Kingsford Smith and Tommy Pethybridge had gone missing in the *Lady Southern Cross* around that time the Englishman obtained more details. He was able to establish the night of the 'big light' was the exact one Smithy was reported to have crashed. The area was close to the island where a wheel from his aircraft was eventually washed ashore. It seemed that someone had witnessed the great airman's final moment.

Mrs Bonney reported the story back to Australia in her next progress release to the *Sydney Morning Herald.*

The weather had improved the following morning and she made Rangoon. To her surprise she was met at the airport by the Italian consul, Carlo Minto. Over a cup of coffee they recalled their last meeting and his fruitless efforts to have her wrecked Moth repaired. At that time the Italian Air Force officer had presented Mrs Bonney with his military pilot's badge as a mark of respect for her gallant effort. She had carried the insignia ever since, only to have it stolen in Camooweal on the present flight. She did not tell him.

The 1300-kilometre crossing to Calcutta was punctuated with frustrating mishaps. Following a refuelling stop at Akyab she had just taken off and reached cruising height when there was a terrific bang. The aircraft started to vibrate badly. The airwoman quickly scanned her engine instruments for a clue to the problem. The oil pressure was normal, the cylinder head correct, the temperature fine, and the engine revs steady. Her engine was operating normally. Then looking up from the instrument panel and peering out of the windscreen, she froze with fear.

Part of the engine cowling was open and flapping in the turbulent slipstream of the propeller. If the hinges came unstuck it would blow straight back and slice into the Klemm rudder and tailplane! She reduced power immediately and slowed back to just above stalling speed. This lessened the violent flapping but the shuddering aircraft was still difficult to control.

Very gently she turned the plane around and headed

back to Akyab. She was worried about the landing. The aircraft was very heavy, with a full fuel load, and the landing would be compounded with the drag of the flapping cowling and the hot thin tropical air. She made a long, straight approach to the tiny landing ground keeping extra speed on as she levelled off over the airfield boundary. She increased the back pressure slightly with the control stick, cut the power, and held off waiting for the wheels to touch. She landed safely on the ground.

Once on land, she soon found the trouble. When the refueller had opened the cowl to check the oil level he had not refastened the latches properly. She kicked herself for not having personally checked it before starting. Such a careless oversight could have led to disaster, had the cowling sprung a few seconds after takeoff when the Klemm was struggling to attain climbing speed. The sudden drag could have brought on a stall.

Mrs Bonney got off again but soon hit bad weather. It was becoming routine. She decided to try an alternate route around the storm. She removed her map from its knee holder and held it up near her face to get a closer look. But as she did so an unseen hand snatched it from her grasp and it was gone. She had held it too close to the open side window and it had been sucked out by the slipstream. She was in a terrible mess.

There was a spare chart packed away in a box on the floor behind her seat but to get at it she had to move some of the emergency equipment stacked in the little cabin. The effort required the flexibility of a contortionist, for she had to twist around, and while still controlling the aircraft with one hand, restack with the other. By the time she located and unlocked the map box she had a large water container in her lap and was minus two fingernails. But she had the map. She thanked her stars for her years of yoga.

After a night's rest in Calcutta she set off across India. She had decided to cross the country as quickly as possible. It was the hot season and she had no desire to linger in its torrid conditions. She was cautioned not to fly in the heat of the day but pressed on regardless.

'I should have listened to the ground staff's advice. I flew from Allahabad to Agra at 200 metres to avoid head winds and turbulence which were terrific up higher. Heat haze reduced the visibility to zero and I was in constant fear of hitting hawks and kites which were everywhere.

'It was so hot in the cockpit that I could not put my hand on the throttle. I eventually had to wrap some cloth around the burning metal. To revive myself I periodically inhaled the vapours of crushed smelling salts and dabbed my skin with *eau de cologne*. The heat can be torrid in the centre of Australia but it has nothing on the Indian sun. I never experienced such conditions anywhere else.

'I had been in the air for three-and-a-half hours and was pushing through a sandstorm when, in the distance, I saw a white dome that seemed to be floating in space. It was the Taj Mahal.'

As Mrs Bonney staggered, exhausted, from her aircraft at Agra's military airport, she nearly tripped over something that seemed stuck to the underside of her shoe. She looked down to discover that the sole was flapping loose attached only by the heel. The searing metal of the Klemm's rudder pedals had melted the gum solution which attached the sole to the shoe.

After an hour in a cold bath she felt much better. The next day, in the cool of dawn, she visited the world's most beautiful building. As she inspected the shrine it crossed her mind that the beautiful Persian wife of Shah Jahan, Mumtaz Mahal, for whom the monument had been built, had enjoyed a freedom rare among the women of India. In some small way, Mrs Bonney thought, her husband Harry had allowed her a similar freedom.

She marvelled at the exquisite mosaics and the beauty of the white marble structure which had taken 20 000 workmen twenty years to build. But breathtaking as it was at close quarters, she would never forget the Taj Mahal as she had first seen it — a great white dome floating above the sandstorm.

Mrs Bonney's progress across India was painfully slow. The intolerable heat and increasingly strong head winds forced her to make a series of short early-morning hops.

The rest of the days she spent on the ground, taking in India. Her unique mode of travel took her to towns far off the beaten track. And at each stopover she could have happily spent weeks exploring. She was in raptures with the country; it was so different and exciting; a land of contrast, with unimaginable wealth and indescribable poverty.

After Agra she flew to Delhi which was busy celebrating the coronation of King George VI. She had been airborne at dusk and from the air had seen the city's principal buildings, fountains, public parks and gardens outlined with thousands of lights. Even the water lilies that floated on the surface of the city's score of lakes concealed glowing lights.

Delhi's celebration was typical of the ostentatious display put on by and for the benefit of the British Raj. England's colonialism was at its peak. In ten years' time the Empire would crumble, with India, led by Mahatma Gandhi being one of the first to break away. But for Mrs Bonney it was still the time of mystical India catering totally it seemed to the Europeans and its own small group of incredibly rich.

In Karachi she was delayed by petty officialdom. Things had not improved during the four years since her last visit. She spent hours with the Persian consul trying to get her visa and a permit to fly over his country. All she received were shrugs of indifference and blank stares. It appeared that the consul was not used to doing, nor cared to do, business with a woman. The consul, his secretary, the postman, his clerk, were all to blame. Everywhere there were delays, arguments and total lack of concern. It was not until two Englishmen living in Karachi heard of her problems and came to her assistance, that she was finally able to leave on the long desert crossing to Cairo.

Next evening at Jask she was badgered by officials. There were questions upon questions; never ending stacks of documents to be signed, raised voices and so it went on. Unable to leave the airport she spent the night in the crew quarters of KLM, the Dutch airline, where she was advised by a fierce looking, but friendly local, 'One-eyed' Ali, to sleep with her revolver under her pillow. He warned her of prowling jackals and wandering villagers.

Between Jask and Bushire she encountered terrible head winds. The 850-kilometre flight took seven hours. At one stage, when she was flying through a gap between two razor-backed mountains she was caught in a violent blast of cross wind. The Klemm drifted sideways towards a sheer rock face. Only a quick and large change in heading kept her away from the mountain.

As she passed the line of ranges and came over the desert, she was again confronted by sandstorms. She had no alternative but to go through them. For several hours she flew on instruments through the dark gritty cloud, always keeping one ear cocked for the first signs of protest from the Klemm's engine. As always it didn't miss a beat. No wonder it had gained such a world-wide reputation for reliability.

The aircraft's compass developed a bubble on this leg of the journey, making its reading inaccurate. She breathed a sigh of relief when she finally intercepted the lonely telephone line leading into Bushire. She had averaged little better than 100 km/h from Jask.

Officials again wanted to quarantine her, but a phone call to the British consul, Sir Trenchard Fowle, did the trick and she was his guest for the night. Nevertheless she was made to leave her flying suit and aircraft keys with the airport manager as security for her return next morning.

She flew to Basra at dawn and landed in time to be entertained to breakfast by a group of RAF pilots stationed in the town. As her aircraft was due for a routine check she asked if the RAF mechanics might help with the job. Skilled servicing was a rarity along the route and it was too good a chance to miss. It was as well she asked.

Two young mechanics, leading aircraftsmen Coppen and Todd, decided to give the Klemm a real going over. Among the other items they checked which are not normally looked at during a standard overhaul, were the leather washers that protected the control cables as they pass down the fuselage. The mechanics noticed that at one point the washers had been worn away by the friction of the metal cables. As a result the control cables had been rubbing against metal. Four of the six wire strands of the rudder cable had broken. The two remaining wires were also starting to fray. A few more hours in the air and Mrs Bonney would have lost rudder control. The mechanics also found that a vital bolt in the undercarriage system had sheared. One heavy landing and it would have collapsed.

'I can never be sufficiently grateful to those two young men. They fixed both faults and in fact gave me the piece of frayed wire as a memento. I took it back to show my husband how close I came to eternity. I counted that day in Basra as one of the luckiest of my life.'

That night she was invited to a moonlight picnic at Qurna, 100 kilometres away on the banks of the Euphrates. It was said to be the site of the original Garden of Eden. There the party was shown a rotten tree limb lying on the ground and surrounded by a concrete wall about a metre thick. They were told it was part of the original apple tree where Adam and Eve had come to grief. Mrs Bonney had her doubts.

As she left each place along her route, the airwoman was finding it increasingly difficult to repack her aircraft. The temptations of the markets were too great, and at most stopovers she had purchased some small memento — a sari here, a pair of ornate slippers there, pearls, carved ivory, silver jewellery and so it went on. Individually each item was tiny and almost weightless, but collectively they were a problem. Her cabin space was already taken up with emergency equipment, food, water, baggage, tools, spare parts and numerous items vital to the flight. Now with the additional weight and bulk of her souvenirs the rear of the cockpit was starting to resemble an aerial bazaar.

She was also having trouble finding room for her washing line! Because of her limited wardrobe, she had made it a habit to do her washing during stopovers. Often this meant leaving next morning with clean but soaking clothing. So, prior to takeoff, she rigged up a clothesline in the cockpit and hung out the washing! She must have looked quite a sight and been the subject of some raucous laughter, as she took off, sitting at the controls with her white helmet and goggles, and her line of washing trailing behind in the slipstream. But Mrs Bonney wouldn't have cared a bit. It was more important that she have a crisp clean outfit at her next stopping place.

By the time she left Baghdad the weight problem was critical. She had taken on an extra hand-tooled copper lamp and an exquisite coffee urn, deciding that since she was nearing Cairo she would clear the cabin, and ship her purchases back home.

Her compass was still giving her trouble as she crossed the desert between Baghdad and Cairo. In such a featureless area it was imperative that her dead reckoning compass course be accurate so when she identified Rutbah Wells with tracks branching out in all directions, she decided to land and ask which track she should follow in case her compass became even more inaccurate. She landed safely and with her engine still ticking over, she parked near the airport building. An official came over to her and gave her directions, but then insisted that she shut down and have her documents inspected and pay fees. Officialdom and money again; bribes disguised as fees. She waited until the man had moved away, then gunned the motor, swung around, and took off leaving the pettifogging official gasping in her dust. It wasn't the money, it was the hours of time wasting she wanted to escape.

She crossed Amman, staggering to 2500 metres to clear the mountains. A few more purchases and she might not have made it. As it was she had difficulty in gaining sufficient height in the heat. Over Palestine the glare of the desert was replaced by the sight of rich green cultivation. After enduring the searing brightness of the sun on sand it seemed almost like wearing a cool, green eyeshade.

From Palestine she flew out over the Sinai desert. Her next real landmark was the Suez Canal. As she crossed de Lesseps' miracle it seemed little more than a blue crack in the sand. Eight-and-a-half hours after leaving Baghdad she saw the pyramids on the outskirts of Cairo. When she landed at the busy airport, taxied in, and closed down her engine, Mrs Bonney sat quietly in her cabin for a moment. With understandable satisfaction she realised that she had just become the first Australian to fly from Australia to Egypt. She savoured the feeling for a moment, then remembered with a jolt that she had only just passed the half way point of her flight. After ninety-eight hours crammed in the cockpit of *My Little Ship* II, she still had to face another ninety hours over the wilderness of Africa before she reached Cape Town. It was a sobering thought.

10
Bravo, Intrepid Airwoman

While Mrs Bonney spent a week in Cairo, *Courier Mail* readers in Brisbane were catching up with news of her latest adventures. She had sent off a long article to the Australian newspapers telling of her flight from Karachi and, as usual, had played down the difficulties of the flight and wrote mostly of the places and people she had seen.

While Mrs Bonney was in Cairo, an article appeared in one of the newspapers criticising her refusal to give any more than sketchy details to the local press. It insinuated that she was receiving full backing from the Australian press on a flight of little significance. The writer suggested that a speed record was necessary to make such a flight of any importance. The journalist totally ignored, or possibly didn't realise, that no one before her had made such a flight.

Another publication was quick to come out with an article in the airwoman's defence.

'It is true that the lady has a contract to write for a syndicate of newspapers, but all the "backing" she is receiving is scarcely enough to buy spare parts. Her real expenses are being found by her husband, a Queenslander of substance. The flight is no stunt but a carefully planned enterprise showing the possibilities and advantages of the new form of foreign travel. Mrs Bonney has gone about it in a most methodical way. She keeps not only a record of the incidents of her journey but also of facts likely to help future air travellers. And those who invite her to dinner entertain no apologetic apparition in oil-smeared slacks, but a daintily dressed, pleasant spoken Australian woman, as careful of her appearance as she is of her machine.'

The washing line had obviously paid off!

Her week in Cairo was spent with the Australian high commissioner, Colonel Hughes, and his wife. They showed her around while she waited for all the formalities to be completed for her flight south. Luckily she already had her clearance to fly over the Sudd. When she had been planning the flight in Australia, the Egyptian Government had refused permission for her to fly solo over the vast swamp. The Sudd, the dregs of Africa and the backwash of the Nile, is a huge expanse of floating vegetation that from the air has the appearance of an endless carpet of rich green velvet.

Captain Johnson, head of Australia's Department of Civil Aviation had personally written to the Egyptian Government on her behalf. He told them that Mrs Bonney was an experienced pilot who had made many long solo flights over equally hazardous country in single-engined aircraft. He was confident of her ability and asked that they waive the regulations in her case. The head of Egypt's aviation department had obliged.

Among other regulations, the authorities in Cairo warned her to keep well clear of 'Queen Bees' over Egypt. They were painted a bright yellow to make them easier to spot the regulation stated. For one moment Mrs Bonney looked at them askance. They were having her on. She conjured up a hilarious picture of aircraft darting all over the place avoiding large yellow insects. Or maybe it was some wild Arabic method of producing honey. She recalled the Aboriginal method of finding honey. The Aborigines caught a bee and attached a tiny piece of down to it, then released it and followed it to the hive — but to paint one yellow, that was just too much. She was quite relieved to learn the 'Queen Bees' were radio-controlled aircraft used by the RAF squadrons based in the Middle East.

On 6 June 1937, she set off on the second half of the flight. The most difficult and hazardous part of the flight lay ahead. Aviation facilities were virtually nonexistent over much of Africa. Few aircraft travelled the vast continent.

It seemed strangely spacious in her cockpit with the removal of her pile of souvenirs. They had been forwarded by sea to Australia. Her course followed the narrow green ribbon of the River Nile with its strip of lush green cultivation on either side. Beyond it as far as the eye could see, was uninterrupted desert.

Thirty minutes after takeoff the needle of the oil pressure gauge began to fluctuate. Either there was a problem with the engine's oil system, or the gauge was faulty. In either case she could not risk carrying on. Khartoum was twelve hours ahead and there was nowhere she could get it fixed *en route*. She turned back for Cairo.

Increasing low cloud and dust haze made it very difficult to locate the airport when she returned to the city. She circled several times before she picked up the large open field.

After landing, she was rushed by angry Egyptian officials demanding to know why she had circled the city when she had been permitted only to leave and go south. They were not the slightest bit interested in her explanation for returning or her problem in locating their field. They were quite sure she had been on some clandestine aerial mission. One particularly unpleasant individual told her that she might have her pilot licence suspended.

Mrs Bonney realised that if she got her back up and started to argue she would get nowhere with the paranoid officials. They seemed to take delight in the opportunity to badger the hapless woman.

'I had learned when I struck this kind of stupid officiousness to keep my temper, and agreed that I was in the wrong. With reluctance and bad grace they accepted my apology.'

Fortunately the oil problem was easily fixed and after two hours she was allowed to leave. Four hours later she landed at Luxor. During her stopover she visited the Valley of the Kings and Tutankhamen's Tomb.

Next day she had left Egypt and entered the Sudan. Customs and diplomatic formalities were conducted at the little town of Wadi Halfa.

After a five-hour flight in good weather she reached Khartoum. She had been warned when leaving Luxor to watch out for 'haboobs', terrifying black dust storms that rise to 3000 metres over the desert. To mix it with one of them meant certain death she had been told. Luckily there had been none on the flight.

The city of Khartoum had been immortalised fifty years earlier when General Gordon and his men were massacred by the Mahdi's force. On flying over the city, Mrs Bonney saw the centre was laid out like a huge Union Jack and that all the streets converged on one central point. She later discovered that General Gordon's tomb stood in the centre. It made an inspiring memorial to the city's colonial martyr.

The Khartoum airfield was well organised and with good facilities. It was a stopping point for Imperial Airways and a squadron of RAF aircraft was based there.

On the five-hour flight to Malakal next day Mrs Bonney finally felt that she was in Africa. The desert had given way to a broad flat expanse of veldt. Way below her she saw herds of wild game; zebra, giraffe, hartebeest, gazelle, running wild in their natural habitat. It was too much of a temptation. She dropped down to a few metres from the ground and indulged herself with some low flying.

At Malakal she spent hours with the local district commissioner preparing a strip map for the 700-kilometre flight to Juba. It was a featureless section of the country which she realised would be difficult to navigate. Juba was a tiny town with no real distinguishing features nearby. She could not afford to merely set a compass course and hope to hit the town. She must keep a close watch on her position all the way. To compound the problem, official aviation weather forecasts were unobtainable and the suggested information about the winds would be little more than an educated guess.

Once on her way, everything went well for the first hour-and-a-half but then she began to have trouble locating the few insignificant landmarks shown on the map. There were tracks on the ground all right but their number and direction bore no resemblance to those shown on the map. She had used a lot of extra fuel trying to pick up a recognisable feature, and after circling for some time, she decided to return to Malakal, refuel, and try again later.

She was only a few metres up, approaching to land in hot turbulent conditions, when the aircraft entered a sudden downdraught. With her air speed low, probably too low for the conditions, she was unable to recover and the Klemm stalled onto the ground with a terrific thump. Another gust of wind caught the aircraft and it groundlooped. For a moment she thought it would turn over, but *My Little Ship* II finally came to a stop amid a cloud of dust and with its tail down in a strange attitude.

Thoroughly shaken, the airwoman clambered down from the cabin and walked back around the aircraft. The reason for its unusual attitude was obvious. The metal tail skid was missing. It had been torn out of the wooden fuselage longeron. She checked the wood and saw it was cracked, and worse still it seemed rotten. Pieces crumbled away in her hand. She recalled the warning of the RAF mechanics in Basra who had told her that some of the Klemm's wooden structure was reaching the end of its useful life and should be replaced.

She was preparing to send a message to Khartoum when she heard the sound of aircraft engines. Looking up she saw three RAF biplanes preparing to land. The pilots came over to meet her, and after inspecting the damage told Mrs Bonney that it would be impossible to repair the aircraft. She would have to ship it back to Khartoum to the RAF maintenance section. They were on their way to Juba and promised to help when they returned in three days.

Meanwhile, Mrs Bonney organised for the Klemm to be shipped by barge down the Nile. A river boat was expected in a couple of days and would tow it to Khartoum. The aircraft was manhandled from the airfield to the river bank. A large flat-topped barge was moored close in to the low-lying shore and the crippled aircraft was inched up a pair of wooden planks and onto the deck by sweating natives.

Once on board, the wings were removed and folded back along the fuselage. A rough, wooden, canvas-covered hangar was built for protection.

A week later the frustrated airwoman was still awaiting the arrival of the paddle steamer. Word came that it was stuck on a mud bank further up-river. She had sent messages back to Australia in an effort to ensure that no wildly inaccurate stories appeared in the press. She was confident that her husband would not be jumping to the wrong conclusions.

For once the press was kind. They reported the facts then gave lengthy coverage to her report of life among the local Shilluk tribe.

She was fascinated by their appearance and customs.

'When I had heard that the riverboat was stuck in the mud I was told that in Africa nothing ever turned out as planned. The locals had accordingly developed a philosophy. I set about trying to acquire some of it. To fill my time I spent the days examining in detail the lifestyle of the local native tribes.

'I was fascinated by their appearance. The men dressed in a piece of henna-coloured material reaching from shoulder to knee. The garment was worn tied over one shoulder. Their hair was usually henna coloured to match, and matted together with powdered brick mixed with oil. A quick look suggested a skull cap, heavily fringed and beaded. Sometimes the hair was dressed in a fan shape or with two discs on either side, rather like two cabbage leaves, one laid on either side of the head.

'It was a strange sight to see these dandies swaggering in twos and threes along the roads or gossiping in the shade of the trees. In contrast to the "elegants" were the workers who wore shorts, singlets and turbans. Curiously I saw few women during my stay. I suppose they were at home in the nearby villages preparing the food for their swaggering lords and masters.'

Mrs Bonney found, with delight, that the local store

carried a range of Australian tinned and dried fruits. Before she left Malakal she had persuaded the owner to order tinned meats and tomato sauce from Australia.

Finally after a ten-day wait the word flashed around town that the boat was coming. Mrs Bonney hurried down to the wharf to find it crammed with chattering, grinning Massai tribesmen and Shilluk dandies. It was the big day of the month and they came in their droves to see the boat arrive. To her amazement she saw not one boat, but five; three abreast and two astern tied closely together in roped formation.

Finally, looking more like a floating market place than a small flotilla, the boats, crammed with poultry, cattle, boxes of fruit, baskets of vegetables, as well as noisy tribesmen and vociferous crews, lurched off down the upper reaches of the Nile to Khartoum.

'Among my fellow passengers were English civil servants and their wives heading home on annual leave.

'All the time I had been in Africa I had been impressed with the particularly fine type of Englishman in the government service. Once a year, I was told, new blood was sent to the outposts. The new arrivals were on probation and only those with the highest qualifications were sent to the Sudan. In its climate the slightest weakness in a man could lead to the kind of deterioration the British Government would not tolerate.'

In her own inimitable style Mrs Bonney was referring to the age old problem of the British colonial service. Not all the Englishmen joined the 'mad dogs out in the midday sun'. Many preferred the cool shade of their verandahs, while servants topped up their tall glasses with long ice-filled drinks, liberally laced with their favourite brand of poison. Alcoholism was the common 'deterioration' the government discovered among many of its officers.

It took five pleasant days filled with deck games, conversation and non-stop meals to reach Khartoum. The river boat *Omdurman* was fitted out like an ocean liner. Her two top decks were reserved for Europeans, while on the third deck, only just above the water line, were crammed non-Europeans and their baggage.

For those in first class it was morning tea, breakfast, mid-morning snacks, luncheon, afternoon tea, dinner, late night supper. The Sudan railways, who catered for the boat, did them proud. Only once was their slow progress interrupted when at three o'clock one morning they stuck on the mud.

The heat of Khartoum was overpowering. On arrival Mrs Bonney's aircraft had been moved to the RAF base and repairs were underway. But it was a slow job. While in Malakal she had received a cable from the commanding officer, saying he was willing to undertake repairs at Khartoum under normal service conditions, that is if airmen worked in their own time. Though realising this could make for a slow job she was grateful of any help. Without the RAF she would have no hope of getting the Klemm back in the air.

During her stay in Khartoum, the city was hit by a 'haboob', and she experienced, from the safety of her hotel, a salutory lesson as to why pilots should never attempt to fly through the desert whirlwind.

'The haboob hits us quicker than any storm I have ever known,' she reported in the Brisbane *Courier Mail*. 'Outside it was pitch black. Through cracks and keyholes a fine black powder oozed and began to settle everywhere. The wind howled with hurricane force. It lasted about twenty minutes. The blackness gave way to a mustard yellow, and wind's violence increased. Then came the rain, a torrential downpour. When it stopped, the sun was shining again. It was like waking from a turbulent dream.'

She spent much of her two-week wait at the city's Museum of Natural Science. There she was able to make a detailed study of the hundreds of species of African birds on display.

Finally the job was completed. Altogether the tail skid had cost her a month — as long as it had taken to completely rebuild her aircraft following Bang Biang. But by African standards she had been lucky. Without the RAF, her aircraft would have languished forever at Malakal.

She waited in Khartoum an extra two days in the hope of meeting Amelia Earhart, whom she had heard was due any moment. The American airwoman with her navigator, Fred Noonan, was attempting to set a new round the world record in her twin-engined Lockheed Electra. However, with no firm word of the Lockheed, Mrs Bonney finally decided to leave on 10 July. She missed her by one day.

She retraced her flight to Malakal where for the second time she had troubles at the aerodrome. The area had recently been drenched with heavy rain, and while taxiing up to put her aircraft in the shelter of the only building around, the wheels became bogged in deep mud. There was no one around to help her and she was forced to resort to using engine power to unstick. She opened the throttle wider and wider, but still the Klemm refused to budge. Then suddenly it lurched out of the mud's sticky grasp and shot forward. She closed the throttle immediately and pulled up, but not before the wing hit a guy wire, which cut deeply into the plywood covering.

She spent the next two hours patching the damage in pouring rain beneath an umbrella. Next morning the Malakal jinx continued. She had only just taken off for Juba when the note of the Gipsy engine took on a new and ominous sound. The instruments indicated nothing amiss but she knew for certain that something was radically wrong. Once again she landed and inspected the engine. She discovered the exhaust gasket had burnt out. Luckily she had a spare with her and was ready to take off an hour later.

It was the third time lucky to Juba. She followed a different route to the one she had become lost on a month earlier. She had been carefully briefed by the RAF pilots, who knew the area like the backs of their hands, having been called on to search for several aircraft missing *en route* to Juba. Thankfully Mrs Bonney did not require their services. She cautiously followed the planned route, map reading all the way. It was treacherous forbidding country. A forced landing was out of the question. She saw her first herd of elephants and celebrated by circling low over them. She was wildly excited but was surprised that the huge beasts stood their ground and did not stampede with fright at her engine noise.

When she reached Juba, she flew low to announce her arrival and then spent another hour searching for game in the local area, then landed and headed for the hotel.

She could not resist the temptation of an opportunity to see the wild animals at close stationary quarters, and jumped at an invitation to a one-day safari by a group of European buffalo hunters. Every time they sighted game the excited Australian woman was all for getting out of the car to take photographs, but her companions had other ideas in mind. It wasn't until they sighted buffalo that she was allowed out, and only then to shin up a tree while they made the kill. Wounded buffalo were extremely ferocious and would charge anyone in sight, they explained. On the return journey she sighted lots more game but the one animal she most wanted to observe, the lion, was not to be seen.

Next day she made the five-and-a-half hour flight to Kisumu on the shores of Lake Victoria. She was now passing through equatorial Africa with its rough uninhabited jungle where the ground rose slowly to a height of 1500 metres. It looked beautiful from the air but most uninviting if the engine failed. She spent the night in a hotel on the lake.

She made two attempts to get through to Nairobi. Although it was only a distance of 250 kilometres, the mountains rose to 3000 metres. She was beaten back by heavy rain and cloud that completely enshrouded the mountains ahead. On her second attempt, a day later, she was invited by the captain of the bi-weekly Imperial Airways aircraft to follow him through the mountains. All was going well until the airliner entered heavy cloud and did not reappear. She too was forced to enter cloud and fly on instruments for a while. She remembered that only a few weeks earlier an aircraft had crashed into the mountains on a similar flight. The wreck containing the pilot's body had been located a couple of days before she arrived at Lake Victoria.

She gave herself plenty of extra height to clear the mountains, or so she thought, but when she finally broke into the clear she was about thirty seconds away from flying straight into the side of a mountain! For a split second she was paralysed with fear; then she hauled back and over on the control column and turned away. She missed the rock face by no more than fifty metres. It was undoubtedly her closest brush with death. Had the cloud extended that tiny bit further she would have hit the near vertical rock head on.

Fortunately the rest of the route through to Nairobi was clear, but she was unable to catch up with her airline escort now far ahead. As she wended her way towards her destination she tried to figure out how she had come so close to death. She reckoned she should have been at least 400 metres above the range. Surely the maps were not wrong. Besides she had checked with the Imperial Airways pilot.

When she landed at Nairobi she talked immediately to the ground engineer. He could only think of one answer. He checked her altimeter. It was reading incorrectly by nearly 800 metres! She had been that much lower than the instrument indicated.

Mrs Bonney spent several days in the Kenyan capital. The lure of Africa was too much. She engaged Captain Gethin, the 'famed white hunter' to take her on an unforgettable three-day safari where she saw every conceivable type of animal, bar lions.

Articles flowed thick and fast back to Australia. This, she said, was the ideal use for light aircraft. Aerial touring, reaching unknown spots off the beaten track and not serviced by public transport.

During the next week she headed slowly south. She restricted herself to short flights of 500-600 kilometres each day. There were two reasons. Firstly the weather: heavy clouds seemed to cover each mountain range she had to cross, and when it was not clouds it was bush fires that cut visibility to near zero. Secondly, she was starting to feel the cumulative effects of the flight. She was approaching her fortieth birthday and it was over four months since she had set out from Brisbane. Admittedly she had not been in the air for one of those months but even waiting for her damaged aircraft to be repaired in the energy-sapping heat of Khartoum had been worrying and enervating.

Two days out of Nairobi she had another nasty experience. She was trying to cross mountains between Dodoma and Mpika, and had staggered to 3500 metres to clear the peaks, when the cloud thickened and she lost sight of the ground. The turbulence threw her aircraft all over the place and one violent jolt almost tore the wings off. She cautiously turned around and returned to Dodoma.

'I arrived back with my tail between my legs, but was cheered to learn that an RAF aircraft and the Imperial Airways plane had both been forced to do the same as I. That did my morale a lot of good.'

Her flight to Broken Hill was decidedly unpleasant. The Klemm was really struggling in the heat to reach a safe altitude. The mountains below looked lethal, just waiting for one mistake or just a small loss of power from her Gipsy engine. When she finally reached the mining town three hours later she was very tired.

She almost came to grief again the next day. She had lined up for takeoff and was just opening the throttle when the starboard undercarriage collapsed, and her aircraft heeled over. The holding bolt had sheared. If it had happened a few seconds later, when she had gathered more speed, the results could have been fatal. Her aircraft was carrying a full load of fuel and would very likely have cartwheeled and exploded. Luckily a local mine engineer was able to fabricate a new holding bolt, and two days later she was safely on her way to Livingstone.

As she moved down towards South Africa she flew over and visited the Victoria Falls and the legendary mystery city of Zimbabwe.

It was a very special day for her on 14 August when she landed at Pretoria, the South African city of her birth. She was given a great reception by the townspeople, and later at a very moving ceremony she was presented with pilot's wings by the Royal South African Air Force as a mark of respect for her pioneering flight. The badge became her most treasured aviation possession, which she wore on special occasions.

The last two days of her long flight to Cape Town took in the diamond mining centre of Kimberley where she was given a civic reception and taken over the mines, and Johannesburg which she remembered best for the most marvellous meal of the journey.

The final six-hour flight from Kimberley over high mountains was quite terrifying. She was forced up to 4000 metres above the snow-covered peaks. Violent air currents made control almost impossible, and over one particularly bad stretch of the Hex River Mountains the Klemm was flung around sideways. The turbulence did not leave her until she arrived over Cape Town.

She landed at Cape Town at 4.55 p.m. on Wednesday, 18 August 1937. Local press described her touch down in the cool sea-level air as 'perfect', and carried the headlines: 'Bravo Mrs Bonney — intrepid airwoman', and 'Australia and the Union at last joined by air'.

As Mrs Bonney relaxed at the Queens Hotel she totalled up the hours and distances in her pilot log book. The Queensland airwoman had flown a staggering 29 000 kilometres in just under 211 flying hours.

Before she sailed for home a week later, she had one more trip to make; this time by car to the Kruger Game Sanctuary. As she drove slowly round a quiet bend in the road, she finally saw a family of lions lazing in the sun. She could now return home satisfied. She had at last seen the creature that to her epitomised the Africa over which she had flown — magnificent but dangerous.

11
The War Years

Mrs Bonney and her aircraft returned to Australia by sea. On her arrival in Cape Town the Klemm had been thoroughly inspected and found to be in need of a major overhaul. The long flight had taken its toll on both woman and machine. Mrs Bonney had at one stage considered disposing of it in South Africa, and purchasing a new aircraft on her return to Australia, but had realised she had become too attached to her German monoplane. They had done so much together that the aircraft had become a part of her life. Furthermore, there had been no great advance in aircraft design, and though there were a few faster touring aircraft on the market she had little to gain from them. Great speed was not necessary for the future flights she envisaged.

Back in Australia, her South African flight received little more than passing recognition. She settled quickly back into Brisbane life. Her husband Harry was still an inveterate golfer and she filled her time with local flying, looking after their home and tending her garden.

By the beginning of 1938 she was planning her next flight. This time she had decided to head east to London. But as her Klemm did not have the range for a trans-Pacific crossing, and she would not have attempted such an undertaking in a single-engined aircraft, she looked for a route within their joint capabilities.

She eventually decided to follow in Francis Chichester's footsteps. When the Englishman had crashed in Japan he had planned to reach England by way of Alaska, America, and the Atlantic Ocean. The Australian woman saw it as an ideal flight. It would combine everything she wanted. She would end her flight in America, however, and continue to London by boat. The challenge of distance and difficulty, and the knowledge that it would be a 'first', appealed to her. She could indulge her passion for aerial touring, demonstrating the new and exciting role for light aircraft.

The thought of visiting Japan *en route* appealed to her in particular. Her love of plants and flowers had remained undiminished through the years. She had occasionally come across exquisite specimens of the traditional Japanese art of bonsai, and the miniature plants and shrubs, many scores of years old, had fascinated her. She was intrigued by the infinite care, patience and strict adherence to the artistic rules and disciplines that were involved in their culture, and hoped the flight would give her an opportunity for a brief but close study of the plants.

She had discussed her plans with her husband, and as always he had enthusiastically given his support. As long as she was not going for a speed record, he felt secure in the knowledge that his wife would not be forced into taking unnecessary risks such as pushing on through bad weather.

However, on a night early in 1939, Mrs Bonney's dream vanished amid the fire and smoke that destroyed the Qantas Number 2 Hangar at Archerfield. *My Little Ship II* was one of a number of aircraft that were incinerated as the building burnt to the ground. The fire brigade was helpless to prevent it and could do little more than control the holocaust from spreading to other buildings. Fed by the high octane fuel exploding from aircraft fuel tanks, the fire lit up the sky and could be seen for kilometres around. Next morning all that remained was a smouldering ruin. Not one recognisable part of the Klemm's airframe remained.

Mrs Bonney continued local flying in hired aircraft, but the trip was off until she could purchase a new machine. Before she could do so the second World War intervened.

In the early part of the war she joined other civil flyers

in offering her expertise to the government. She delivered a light aircraft to one of the RAAF flying schools that were mushrooming all over the country, and was keen to help with the Empire Training Scheme, which gave tens of thousands of Allied pilots their flying training in Australia and Canada, far removed from bomb-ravaged England. But from the outset of the war Mrs Bonney found that there was no part for women pilots to play in such a scheme.

It was different in England. Civilian pilots, men too old for active service, and women, were encouraged to join the government organised group, Air Transport Auxiliary, which spent the war years delivering military aircraft to airfields throughout the country. The group's contribution allowed service pilots to be released from ferrying duties to go on active service. Among the ATA's many well-known women pilots, was pioneer airwoman Amy Johnson. In fact, she lost her life early in the war while on duty. She was caught in appalling weather while ferrying a twin-engined Airspeed Oxford, and forced to bail out over the Thames Estuary. She was seen coming down in her parachute and a boat raced to her rescue. However, on hitting the water she became tangled up in the shroud lines of her parachute and dragged under. By the time she was pulled from the water she had drowned. It was a tragic end for one of the world's most daring and courageous pioneer aviators.

Mrs Bonney found her own way to help the nation's war effort, becoming a Queensland organiser for the Women's Voluntary National Register, an Australia-wide organisation which was the brain child of General Sir Thomas Blamey. Though it appeared rather mundane compared with flying, it was nevertheless an important and time consuming contribution. The WNVR mustered the women of Australia for war. It was the medium through which the air force and the army could recruit women to go into uniform. But probably the organisation's greatest achievement was to rally tens of thousands of voluntary workers to perform countless jobs on behalf of the war effort. Volunteer typists, secretaries, transport drivers, mechanics, librarians, canteen workers, seamstresses, nursing assistants, social workers, farm workers, and others were supplied by the WNVR.

Mrs Bonney travelled the State organising new branches. She worked tirelessly throughout the war. Women were at last proving their capabilities! She later received official recognition for her national emergency quilt and mattress scheme, in which she organised thousands of women to manufacture these unobtainable items to equip the air raid shelters being constructed in every Australian city.

It was during the early stages of the war that Mrs Bonney finally decided, regardless of her husband's feelings, that she must learn to drive. It seemed ridiculous that she could fly half way around the world yet still was unable to take one of the two family cars to the top of the road.

Her decision was re-enforced one day by a small but significant exercise of her imagination. Mrs Bonney was waiting to cross a Brisbane street when a formation of aircraft passed overhead. Like her, a group of children standing nearby craned their necks to watch the fast moving warplanes.

'I don't know why, but it suddenly crossed my mind that if those aircraft had been enemy planes about to bomb Brisbane, and I had been driving a car rather than being on foot, I could have swept up those little children and driven them away to safety. As a non-driver I would have been unable to do anything to help. I decided at that moment I would learn to drive.'

She did so, and in typical fashion took driving lessons in secret. It was not as difficult to cover up as the flying lessons had been. And when the time came to reveal her new skill to her husband she did so with her own inimitable flair.

One morning, after they had driven together to the golf course, she remarked that it was a pity she would have to sit at the club all day until he finished playing. Harry Bonney agreed, saying it would be much more convenient if she could chauffeur him, and use the car for the rest of the day. He had got out of the car to open her door. Now was the time to set him up, she thought.

'What a pity I don't have a car,' she tossed it in flippantly.

'My dear,' her husband confidently quipped back, 'there's the car right here. If you can drive it, it's yours.'

Then Harry Bonney shaking his head in amazed disbelief, saw his wife slip into the driver's seat, start the motor, ease it into gear, and take off up the road. After all those years he should have known!

12
Healing the Wound

By the time the aircraft industry moved back into the production of light touring aircraft after the second World War Mrs Bonney was fifty years old and had flown only a handful of hours in the previous seven years. It was too late to start again.

Sadly she was forced to acknowledge she had all the symptoms that signal the end of even the best professional pilot's flying career — slowing of the reflexes, loss of close vision, and a tendency towards deafness.

Had the war not forced a seven-year break late in Mrs Bonney's flying life, she might well have carried on through the 'fifties. But she was smart enough not to let her emotional wishes cloud the issue and prevent her making a decision based on carefully rationalised facts. The break had been too long for her to easily bridge the gap. With re-training and practice she might regain her previous standard but she knew it was too late in life to really enjoy the rigours of aerial touring again. It was time to find another consuming interest, one that was not likely to be curtailed by advancing years.

It was then she began her long love affair with bonsai. After an initial group holiday in Japan, she returned four times between 1959 and 1964 to study under two of Japan's most revered teachers of bonsai. Her first teacher Yoshimura allowed her to sit in on his classes until there was a vacancy. She worked hard to master the intricate and disciplined art. Later, under Kawamoto, she studied bonsai in each of the four seasons.

Through him, Mrs Bonney gained her prized bonsai

teaching diploma, one of very few Australians at the time to possess one. At the invitation of Professor Joyce Ackroyd, she lectured in bonsai to Japanese students at the University of Queensland. She was also in demand to appear on television on the subject which was just beginning to capture Australians' imaginations. Today her bonsai nursery is one of the most extensive in the country.

Her love for travel had not declined. And though she was no longer able to tour by air she still longed to visit the out of the way corners of the earth. In 1963, at the age of 65, she achieved a childhood dream by visiting South America. But not for her the tourist route. As one might have expected she headed for a spot where few tourists and white people had been. Accompanied by a guide and Peruvian Indian bearers she headed for the backwaters of the Amazon River to spend several weeks among the Yagua Indians. They went first by launch, then dugout canoe and finally tramped kilometres on foot through hills and jungle to reach the village.

She studied their way of life, customs and traditions closely. She was intrigued with the women and for hours she watched them manufacture the twine that they used to make their sleeping hammocks and seats. Years of rolling the rough fibre constantly against their thighs had left the skin thick with callus.

She joined the men, crossing the slippery logs that forded the protective streams surrounding the village, barefoot. Once in the jungle they demonstrated their unerring accuracy with the curare-tipped darts of their blow pipes. To her dismay they used giant jungle butterflies as targets.

When she returned home, tucked in her case were decorative jewellery made of toucan feathers, strings of jingling seed pods used at ceremonial dances, and other mementos of 'her' South America.

Harry Bonney died in 1965, after a long battle with cancer. With her husband's death she felt it was time to leave their Bowen Hills home. Somehow, it now was too large and too full of memories for her to continue on there. She had built a weekend retreat on a hill overlooking the Pacific at Miami on the Gold Coast. With extensions it was the ideal place for her to live.

The extensions included a complete Japanese wing added on to the house. Though only small it contained traditional living, sleeping, cooking and washing areas. The interior was built of materials she collected while visiting Japan and was furnished in the traditional manner. Beneath the house she had a nursery built to accommodate her growing collection of bonsai.

The rest of her home was filled with treasured furniture and mementos of a lifetime of travel. A special breezy spot in the house was reserved for her two most treasured mementos, the white parrots Hitch and Hike. They had been presented to her as chicks on Mornington Island during her flight around the missions in 1935. From then on their raucous voices and carefully trained and rehearsed antics dominated her home life.

As the years passed she slipped into retirement, quite forgotten by the rest of Australia. She maintained close ties with her friends. She attended her local church and regularly visited those in hospitals and old people's homes. The constant attention demanded by her bonsai and her garden left no time to be bored. She had cut all ties with the world of flying except for occasional contact with the Australian Women Pilots Association.

However, in 1973, interest in her awakened following the publication of the article on her flying career in the Brisbane *Sunday Mail*. During the next few days letters and phone calls from long-lost friends, acquaintances and people who simply 'remembered', indicated she had not been totally forgotten. One call came from a man with a decidedly English voice, who lived just down the road.

'I don't know whether you remember me Mrs Bonney. My name's Jerry Randall. I was the one who inspected your aircraft and gave you the certificate of airworthiness when it was repaired in Calcutta in 1933.'

She had found another old friend and a new neighbor.

As further stories about her appeared, Mrs Bonney found more and more old friends, and just people who remembered her flights. Encouraged, she began to move out of her self-imposed aviation exile and start attending numerous aviation functions. In no time she was a very special guest, and often guest of honour, presenting air race trophies here, opening a new aviation museum there, and attending air pageants etc.

While attending an annual conference of the Australian Women Pilots Association she came across another link with the past.

Following her England flight she had presented a trophy to be awarded annually as an encouragement to a deserving British woman pilot. Known as the Bonney Trophy it took the form of a map of Australia with pearls inset at each of the landing points of her 1932 round-Australia flight.

At the conference Mrs Bonney met a representative of the British Women Pilots Association who gave her exciting news. The trophy was still being awarded each year, and had recently been presented to a young woman pilot by Prince Charles at a Royal Aero Club dinner.

At least in England her flight was not forgotten!

Time slowly healed the wound left in 1949 when she had written to the director general of Civil Aviation, Sir Richard Williams, enclosing her pilot licence with a note thanking the department for giving her so much assistance on her flights. Recognition and renewed interest in the glorious flying days of the 1930s, finally erased the scar.

The climax of her new life came when the ABC documentary on her life went to air in 1977. *Somehow we almost forgot Mrs Bonney* brought a flood of letters and calls to her Miami home. It also brought a ghost from a tragic moment in her past. George Ditchman, a young trainee in the Qantas workshop during her 1932 'apprenticeship' days, was at a special preview of the television documentary. He presented her with a relic he had rescued from the rubble of the burned out Qantas hangar. Mounted on one of the Gipsy's engine's pistons was the brass compass verge ring belonging to her beloved Klemm *My Little Ship* II.

In 1978 she was an honoured guest of the Australian Government at the official celebrations commemorating the Fiftieth Anniversary of the first trans-Pacific crossing by the men of the *Southern Cross*. She and Nancy Bird were among the first to meet Charles Kingsford Smith Jnr when he landed at Eagle Farm after reenacting his famous father's crossing.

In the same year she was waiting to meet RAF pilot David Cyster when he arrived in Brisbane flying an old Tiger Moth biplane. Cyster had followed her cousin Bert Hinkler's route to Australia in a personal tribute on the Golden Anniversary of the Queensland pilot's epic flight.

Over lunch and for a whole afternoon David Cyster and Mrs Bonney avidly compared notes on their respective flights. Their aircraft had been very similar and they had both used the same airstrips. Cyster said afterwards,

'My Moth was 30 km/h faster than Mrs Bonney's, and it was equipped with radio, navigation aids, and modern instruments. It took me about a month and I didn't crash and have to rebuild my aircraft. And I had a ground party travelling ahead of me to organise everything before I arrived. I can really appreciate just what she went through. Believe me she is a remarkable lady.

'I find it hard to understand how it is, that until I arrived in Brisbane this morning, I had never heard of Mrs Bonney,' he added.

Epilogue to First Edition

It seems incongruous that Mrs Bonney waited all those years before she finally received some recognition for her flights, from other pilots.

Scant attention was paid by her peers in Australia at the time of her flights. The reason may well be that she was a woman. Flying was a man's world in which female pilots were tolerated but not generally encouraged. Some were considered a bit of a laugh, particularly those who merely employed their own personal pilots, and hoped, as passengers, to bathe in the reflected glory of record breaking. These 'record-breakers' included women like sixty-year-old Princess Loewenstien-Wertheim, who wanted to be the first woman to fly across the Atlantic. She flew into oblivion dressed in purple riding breeches and jacket, yellow boots and a black toque hat, and seated in her favourite wicker chair behind her pilots, Dan Minchin and Leslie Hamilton, when her Fokker Universal *St Raphael* vanished in mid-ocean.

Millionairess, the Honorable Elsie Mackay, heir to the P&O steamship fortune, and her pilot Ray Hinchliffe, also disappeared without trace over the same ocean.

There were others, but only a few were seriously involved with flying. Amelia Earhart, wife of publishing magnate G. P. Putnam; glamorous German socialite, Eli Beinhorn; and of course Australian silvertail, Lores Bonney, were among the 'serious few'.

The indifferent attitude of Australian men in the 'thirties to these serious few was not unique. But it lasted much longer in Australia than in Europe and America. In fact, it was from America that the first really significant official recognition of Mrs Bonney's achievements came. In 1955 she was invited to attend a ceremony at the St Francis Atrio Mission in Riverside, California. The mission had some years before instituted a Famous Flyers' Wall, honouring the 'greats' of aviation. The names of the aviators of the world had been engraved on metal pilot wings, and placed on permanent display. Mrs Bonney was in attendance the day her name was added to the distinguished roll that read like a 'who's who' of the history of flying.

However, in Australia her name remained outside the few major books recording our aviation history. To those with whom she shared the thrill of flying, she had been merely a Brisbane housewife who had flown to places, slowly! They failed to recognise that to be first was an enduring record, to be fastest only ensured fleeting recognition, for there would always be another record breaker following.

This fact is borne out time and time again. Most Australians can recall that Bert Hinkler was the first man who flew solo from England to Australia, they know that 'Smithy' was first across the Pacific, and probably that Lindbergh was the first pilot to fly the Atlantic. But except for aviation buffs, few would recall the second person to make those flights even though they did it faster.

And if one looks at the time taken by the *Southern Cross* to fly the 11800-kilometre Pacific crossing, it was not a feat of speed. The flight encompassed ten days of which eighty-three hours was actually spent in the air, and that with a crew of four including two pilots! The first circumnavigation of the world in 1924 by a team of United States' Army aircraft took 175 days, of which only fifteen-and-a-half were spent in the air. Yet those flights have made history.

When viewed in this light Mrs Bonney's lack of speed was unimportant. The fact was that as a woman she failed to catch the enduring imagination of the Australian public. Perhaps, had she ended, rather than started, her flight in Australia it might have been different. But in the long run one comes back to the old problem; lack of interest by a male-dominated and oriented profession in the achievements of a woman.

Mrs Bonney has earned her place as a pioneer of light aircraft long distance flying. Like the other early flyers she also had her own unique way of doing things. Hinkler flew with a minimum of fuss. 'Smithy' was a showman to the core. Ulm was a 'gentleman flyer' with a shrewd business sense. Mrs Bonney flew with style, but not for any other reason than that it was her life. It was not easy in the rough and tumble world of windy cockpits, oily engines and dusty airstrips. But she managed always to attract the attention of fashion writers whether climbing from her aircraft after a long flight or attending a select social gathering in Cloncurry, Cairo or Cape Town.

The Cairo journalist who told his readers not to expect 'an apologetic apparition in oil-smeared slacks,' hit it right on the head. To her a woman's appearance at all times was every bit as important as strict adherence to all the other social niceties.

The intricate details of her wardrobe seemed to totally absorb the reporters who haunted the airfields. In fact, every detail of her stylish life was microscopically examined, from her home, and its exquisite furnishings, to her Persian cat, Cloudy, her pekinese, Ping, and her pet hare, Wee Sing. It was a pity they didn't bother to focus on her achievements, with the same attention to detail.

Mrs Bonney's 'style' extended far beyond the world of flying. She had been born into a family whose background, German on her father's side and English on her mother's, had been part and parcel of the strictly coded society of Europe during the grand Victorian era.

It was only natural that her father should insist that his daughter be educated in the manner of a young lady from a wealthy European family, despite the fact that they had recently settled in Australia. His influence on her, and that of the Victoria Pensionat, was to be lasting.

The importance placed on manners, good taste, conversation, music, the social graces, the indefinable qualities that went into the making of a 'lady' in the traditional sense, were indelibly ingrained in her make-up. In European society she would have been called a 'socialite'. In Australia her workmates in the Qantas repair shop called her a silvertail. It was really the same.

When reading the journals she kept during her flights, recording not only her hours in the air, but also impressions and thoughts about the places she visited, it becomes easy to picture Mrs Bonney as an aerial Aunty Mame.

Today the airwoman of style has been grounded for over thirty years. But other than to hang up her goggles, she has changed very little. She remains a 'lady' from a vanished era, coping very well with a changed world while still retaining what she values of the old one.

To those Australians of the 1970s fortunate enough to know her well, Mrs Bonney is champagne and pearls, afternoon teas, copper-plate thank-you notes, exquisitely served luncheons, birds, gardening, bonsai, and love and concern for her country.

Yet among it all still lurks the rebel with her lifelong love for breaking out of the constrictions of accepted society norms. Mrs Bonney, the airwoman, did it in 1930 with the aid of instructor Charles Matheson, and today, if she were as young in body as she remains in spirit, she would join the new aviation rebels, the hang-glider pilots. She often watches them from the living room of her Miami home as they search for air currents over the nearby headland, and marvels at their ability to emulate a bird in flight.

'It seems as close as man will ever come to real flying,' she remarks wistfully.

And for a brief moment one can imagine her soaring beneath a multi-coloured, para-wing *My Little Ship* III, dressed in a natty little leather outfit made especially for her by her bemused but encouraging husband, Harry.

Terry Gwynn-Jones
Brisbane, 1978

Epilogue to Second Edition

> Mrs Bonney is the last major survivor of the Golden Age of aviation in Australia and possibly the world . . . She is still with us — a precious living legend.
>
> Frank Colyer,
> *Shell Times*, June 1985

'Splendid news about the book. I am sure it will be a great success. Please accept my best wishes. Philip.'

The telegram from Buckingham Palace dated 7 December 1979 was the highlight of the ceremony which launched the first edition of this biography (*Pioneer Airwoman, Rigby*). Appropriately the launch was held at Brisbane's historic Newstead House, a long take-off run from Lores' former Bowen Hills home. It was an emotional affair for the 82-year-old airwoman, listening to the tribute paid her by Senator Kathy Martin, being interviewed and photographed by a flurry of journalists, and finally being handed the telegram from Prince Philip. As one of the guests put it, 'It is almost fifty years too late, but at last it is Mrs Bonney's day.'

The media agreed. A FORGOTTEN WOMAN OF AVIATION FINALLY ARRIVES . . . PILOT HEADS FOR FAME AT LAST . . . THE HEROINE WE ALMOST FORGOT . . . AIR PIONEER WINS RECOGNITION . . . OUR FIRST LADY OF THE CLOUDS . . .the headlines and a score of subsequent book reviews, lionised Lores.

Writing in the Brisbane *Courier-Mail*, Jack Lunn summed it up:

> A fiercely independent spirit that Germaine Greer well might envy catapulted Mrs Lores Bonney into a series of flying adventures that make the Perils of Pauline look tame stuff indeed. While Pauline faced frequent death on celluloid, Lores' adventures — and what whizz-bang adventures — were for real.
>
> And, unlike Germaine Greer, Lores did her thing as a woman at a time — the 1930s — when the word 'liberation' referred to freeing an oppressed populace.
>
> You may have heard of Lores, but chances are that you have not, and this is most unfair. She is a pilot (I doubt whether Lores would like the rather quaint 'aviatrix') who deserves recognition.

Many journalists also chastised Australians for allowing the feats of such a remarkable woman to be forgotten. Both men and women writers blamed male prejudice and patronising attitudes towards women's achievements. Jane Sullivan wrote in the *Age*: 'Perhaps the most exasperating obstacle of all for the Australian airwoman was the apathy and lack of recognition that greeted her exploits, both at the time and fifty years later.'

It would be nice to record that the interest and plaudits resulting from *Pioneer Airwoman* quickly made Lores a permanent national celebrity. However, as with her flights, the excitement soon died away and she seemed destined to return to obscurity.

The breakthrough came in 1980 when the Jacaranda Press, for the first time, included chapters on Australian woman pioneers in one of their Endeavour Reading Programme schoolbooks. Titled *Under the Southern Cross*, the book contained chapters on Elizabeth Macarthur and Lores Bonney. The youth of Australia soon demonstrated Lores would never again be forgotten. Letters began arriving from girls and boys seeking autographs, asking questions, or simply expressing their admiration. School classes conducting projects or writing essays about Lores sent her their work. Deeply touched, she answered every letter in her stylish handwriting.

'The children are so important. I always tell them to choose a goal and pursue it and, when things get difficult, not to give up and to stay cheerful. To emphasise my point I always enclose a copy of my photo standing by my damaged aeroplane in Africa. I point out that even though it seemed my flight was in jeopardy that I am still managing a smile,' she explains.

The reaction from Australian schoolchildren also to some degree helped assuage Lores' life-long disappointment that she and Harry Bonney had been unable to have children of their own. Toowoomba's Fairholme College, where she was asked to plant a 'Bonney Tree', held a competition for the best essay about the airwoman. Lores rewarded the winner with a weekend holiday at her Miami home.

It no longer mattered if older generations still scratched their heads and looked blank when her name was mentioned; or that ill-informed journalists still focussed on Amy Johnson and Amelia Earhart — ignoring one of aviation's last living pioneers on their doorstep. Lores Bonney had bridged the generation gap and Australians of the future will be better informed.

Eventually her daily mail began to include an increasing number of letters from adults. Philatelists sought her advice and sent her copies of first day covers she had carried on her flights . . . other pilots and mechanics from the 1930s wrote about the old days . . . long-forgotten friends and acquaintances re-established contact . . . complete strangers mailed copies of her book to be autographed. Among letters from overseas she was astonished, following a brief illness, to receive a get-well letter from the prime minister of South Africa.

In December 1981, on the fiftieth anniversary of her first long-distance record flight (from Brisbane to Wangaratta), Lores received a most remarkable personal tribute. Dorothy Dean, a 28-year-old schoolteacher and pilot from tiny El Arish in North Queensland, spent her Christmas holidays (and $5000 of her own money) giving Australia a long overdue history lesson. The 150-hour private pilot recreated Lores Bonney's 1932 around-Australia flight.

Her lectern was the cockpit of a small single-engined Cessna 172 aircraft, her classroom the skies, and her students a nation of forgetful Australians. Though Dorothy's cabin monoplane was a far cry from the open cockpit of *My Little Ship* it was, nevertheless, the modern counterpart of Lores' wind-in-the-wires era biplane.

Dorothy explained the motivation for the magnificent gesture on the morning of her departure from Brisbane's Eagle Farm airport. 'Six months ago I read about Mrs Bonney's accomplishments in her biography. I felt something should be done to recognise her contribution to Australian aviation and decided to make this Bonney Jubilee Flight.'

Lores was there to see Dorothy off and present her with the silver brandy flask that she had carried on all her pioneering flights. One naive journalist asked Lores if she was confident that Dorothy could manage to complete the flight. Remembering similar patronising questions from her past, she fixed him with a stern glare, and retorted: 'Young man, her preparation has been superb. She has done everything to ensure success. I have every confidence in her and am delighted she is making the flight. Dorothy is helping lift the status of women . . . out of the kitchen as it were.'

Minutes later Lores detached herself from the crowd. Steadying herself against the propeller of a parked aircraft, and hand-shading her eyes against the morning sun, she watched Dorothy Dean take off. There were tears and a faraway look in her eyes. 'Oh what a wonderful adventure Dorothy is in for,' she said wistfully as the Cessna vanished over the western horizon.

Rather than aim for speed, Dorothy stopped-over at the twenty-one towns and settlements her hero had used as refuelling points. At each, with the help of Apex, she met people who had seen Lores arrive in 1932. She addressed civic gatherings and went on radio and television to tell Mrs Bonney's story. She also presented fifty copies of *Pioneer Airwoman* to local libraries. In the little free time that remained Dorothy haunted museums and newspaper archives collecting photographs and old news clippings of the original flight. With them she made a scrapbook to present to Lores at the completion of the jubilee flight.

Five weeks and 13,000 air kilometres later Dorothy Dean ended her crusade back at Brisbane Airport. As she stepped from the cockpit an emotional Lores placed a lei of orchids around her young counterpart's neck. It was similar to one presented to the pioneer by Harry Bonney in 1932. Lores was momentarily lost for words.

'Thank you. What a wonderful woman you are,' she eventually told Dorothy.

Also present to greet Dorothy Dean and meet Mrs Bonney was the federal member for the local seat of Lilley, Elaine Darling. It was a fortuitous meeting. Since 1979 I had been seeking, with little apparent success, a formal gesture of recognition of Lores Bonney's pioneering achievements by the Australian government. But the lists of proposed recipients for awards was long and choices seemed influenced by more recent achievements. I eventually suggested to Queensland's Regional Director of Aviation, Mike Seymour, that it would be appropriate if a part of the proposed new Brisbane Airport terminal building were named after her. Despite his considerable support, the proposal appeared to be bogged down in Canberra red tape. Elaine Darling offered to help.

Two months later in the House of Representatives, she asked the bemused Minister for Transport, Ralph Hunt, the following question on notice: 'Has his (the minister's) attention been drawn to the outstanding achievements of pioneer Australian airwoman, Mrs Lores Bonney? In view of the lack of recognition accorded Mrs Bonney in contrast to recognition given her in certain other countries, will he give consideration to naming the new domestic airport terminal in Brisbane, or a room in that terminal, in honour of Mrs Bonney?'

In true *Yes Minister* style, an urgent request for a briefing on Mrs Bonney and her achievements came down the bureaucratic pipeline to my desk in Brisbane. With Mike Seymour's support, the minister was provided with an instant backgrounder and glowing recommendations. Elaine Darling's question had cut through the red tape, and a few weeks afterwards it was announced that the VIP room in Brisbane's international terminal building was to be named the Bonney Room — an interim measure until the new domestic terminal was completed.

On 24 September 1982 the Bonney Room was dedicated by the then Minister for Aviation, Wal Fife. It contains maps and photographs, and a life-size photographic wall mural of Lores and *My Little Ship*. Inspecting the plaque which commemorates her flights, Lores told the minister: 'It's fifty years ago today that I took off from a paddock near by father's property at Wangarratta heading for Brisbane during my around Australia flight.'

For a minute they discussed the historic flight before Lores — who had earlier noted an incorrect date on the plaque — bluntly brought the error to the minister's attention. As Mr Fife tried valiantly to cover his embarrassment, she smiled sweetly and said: 'I am sure you will have that corrected won't you?' — fifty years on Lores still knows how to handle bureaucrats.

The Bonney Room has become the venue for the annual Amelia Earhart function held by Zonta — the world-wide women's service club. As Amelia Earhart was one of Zonta's founding members it was appropriate that Zonta's Gold Coast Club made Lores Bonney an honorary life member. In 1983 Zonta's Amelia Earhart function became the setting of a remarkable and moving reunion. It was pure *This Is Your Life*.

Three weeks earlier I had met Captain Russell Tapp

— an early Qantas pilot whose illustrious career went back to 1929. The 85-year-old airline pioneer had just regained his private licence to become the oldest flying pilot in Australia, possibly the world. His single-engined Musketeer was a far cry from the Empire and Catalina flying boats he had commanded during World War II. During conversation Mrs Bonney's name was mentioned and Captain Tapp had told me that, although they had never actually met, he had saved her from a 'spot of bother' during her flight to England in 1933. Based at Camooweal, he was preparing to make the Qantas mail flight to Daly Waters as he watched Lores take off for Darwin. As her DH Moth disappeared over the horizon he realised that it was headed way off course towards the desolate Simpson Desert — instead of the correct route over Daly Waters. Captain Tapp jumped into his biplane and flew off in hot pursuit. He eventually caught up and, by waggling his wings and handsignalling, convinced the endangered airwoman to change course and follow his lead. Several hours later he peeled off to Daly Waters waving to Lores as she continued on to Darwin.

Lores told me that she had accompanied a Qantas plane to Daly Waters but had never mentioned the drama (page 63). I decided that it was time the two finally met, and unbeknown to Lores arranged for Russell to be alongside her at the Amelia Earhart function.

I had been asked to talk to the Zontians about Lores Bonney and, embellishing the tale, I was able to weave in the story of how, but for the quick thinking actions of a young Qantas pilot, she might have become Australia's Amelia — vanishing in mystery out over the uninhabited Simpson Desert. As I recounted the event Lores acknowledged that a Qantas pilot had helped her, agreeing how sad it was that she had never had a chance to meet and thank her unknown helper.

Moments later the audience of dignified Zontians wiped their eyes as Lores Bonney, biting her lip in an unsuccessful effort to hold back the tears, hugged a smiling Russell Tapp. 'It's fantastic, absolutely fantastic. I remember following you but I am still sure I was heading in the right direction all the time,' Lores said. Sadly the newfound friendship was short lived. Soon after that magical day Captain Russell Tapp was killed in a tragic road accident.

In recent years interviews with Lores have appeared in numerous magazines and newspapers. She has been on the *Willesee* show and is a sure-fire media attention-getter at the few functions she attends. "Electronic" Dick Smith, a longtime admirer, landed at Coolangatta specially to meet her while making his around-the-world helicopter flight. She was an honoured guest at Queensland's Royal Flying Doctor Service dinner when Prince Philip was the keynote speaker. Following his address the Prince asked to meet Lores. After shaking hands — a rare gesture in royal circles — Lores returned to her table swearing she would 'never wash this hand again.'

International recognition came from the world's most prestigious aviation museum, the Smithsonian Institution's National Air and Space Museum in Washington DC. The famed air museum requested copies of her biography for their library. Soon after I provided a research dossier on Lores for the museum's archives. Today her photographs are included on the museum's video disk retrievel system and their computers list research material on her life, under BONNEY, LORES (MRS HARRY), AUSTRALIAN PIONEER AIRWOMAN. 'We record and store archival material on all the world's great flyers and are proud to include Mrs Bonney. We could not understand how we had missed her all these years,' one of the curators said. Formal recognition of her achievements came from an Australian museum in 1985 when Sydney's new Powerhouse Museum asked Lores to donate her aviation memorabilia to be displayed when the new building opens in 1988.

Faces from the past still turn up on her doorstep. Early in 1987 she received a call from Melbourne. She recalled the conversation with a gleam in her eye. 'This strange English voice said "Hello Lores this is Rollo Bolton". When I told him I could not remember the name he answered: "How could you forget me. Fifty years ago we lived together for four days in Africa."'

Rollo Bolton was district commissioner of Malakal where she damaged her aircraft (page 145). Following the accident Lores was his house guest while she made arrangements to ship her damaged Klemm up-Nile to Khartoum. Ninety-years-old and living in retirement in England, Rollo was visiting his daughter in Melbourne, where Lores' name came up by pure chance. A week following the phone call the Englishman and his wife arrived on the Gold Coast as guests of Mrs Bonney.

In her 90th year Lores Bonney is physically frail but still a mental powerhouse. A lionhearted spirit, her charm, wit, and magnetism remain. So too does her ability reprove careless young journalists with a withering remark — as one television interviewer recently discovered. Considering that the reporter seemed too concerned with his own patter, Lores asked innocently: 'Am I boring you?'

Journalist Shelly Neller summed her up perfectly in the Brisbane *Daily Sun*: 'She's not only a courageous pioneer pilot but also a charming scallywag . . . she's not short on chat. In private conversation, the dimunitive octogenarian with the pragmatic views, the flirtatious tone, a ready laugh and a great pair of legs, could entertainingly talk the wings off a Jumbo jet'.

Lores was recently asked to help launch the CSR Hinkler Bicentennial Air Race at a ceremony in the Queensland Museum. Other official guests included the Queensland Governor, Sir Walter Campbell, and acting American consul David Seal, a nephew of Charles Lindbergh. The media was out in force. All of Brisbane's television stations, and most of the radio stations and local newspapers were there. When the official ceremonies ended they made a bee-line for Lores. Black cloche hat, smart silk outfit, pearls, and high heels that would have challenged a woman fifty years her junior, still the airwoman with style, she stole the show. Lores held court, surrounded by the media sitting crosslegged at her feet. Cameras were rolling. A dozen outstretched arms held microphones. 'Are the cameras going?' she asked while shrewdly summing up her audience. 'My first flight? That was with Bert Hinkler in 1928. It was in this aeroplane right behind me. Of course you're all much too young to remember him.'

An hour later she was still reminiscing. The cameras, probably out of film, were still rolling. No one wanted to go home — tribute indeed from the normally impatient media. They listened entranced by this living treasure and her memories of aviation's adventuring days. A young reporter obviously hearing about Lores' exploits for the first time, whispered to her neighbour: 'She's amazing. Someone should write a book about her.'

Terry Gwynn-Jones
Brisbane, 1987

Appendix

APPENDIX 1

Details taken from Mrs Bonney's Pilot Log Book
Brisbane-Wangaratta Flight, 26 December 1931.

A single longhand entry states:

> 26.12.31. Solo. Left Brisbane 4.30 a.m. Landed Coffs for 30 mins.
> Sydney 11.30 a.m. Cootamundra 5.15 p.m. Wangaratta 7.20 p.m. Was delayed 45 mins at Cootamundra with throttle trouble.
> Time: 14.30 mins flying for 947 miles.
> Set new Australian record for distance covered in one day.

APPENDIX 2

Details taken from Mrs Bonney's Pilot Log Book Round Australia Flight 1932

DATE	AIRCRAFT Type	AIRCRAFT Reg	JOURNEY	Time in air Hrs	Time in air Mins	REMARKS
15.8.32	DH 60	VH-UPV	Brisbane-Blackall	7	43	Froze. Two forced landings
16.8.32	"	"	Blackall-Cloncurry	3	10	OK
17.8.32	"	"	Clon-Camooweal	3	40	OK
18.8.32	"	"	Cam-Darwin	8	15	OK
20.8.32	"	"	Darwin-Ord River	6	45	Awful trip
21.8.32	"	"	Ord Riv-Halls Creek	4	40	Undercarriage collapse
22.8.32	"	"	Halls Creek-Broome	5	53	Lost three hours
23.8.32	"	"	Broome-Roebourne	4	5	
24.8.32	"	"	Roe-Geraldton	9	5	
25.8.32	"	"	Ger-Moora	2	30	Forced down by weather
26.8.32	"	"	Moora-Perth	1	15	Shocking weather (spar discovered)
4.9.32	"	"	Perth-Loongana	6	11	Landed. Too dark
5.9.32	"	"	Loongana-Ceduna	5	35	
6.9.32	"	"	Ceduna-Parafield	4	5	
8.9.32	"	"	Parafield-Northfield		10	Forced landing
16.9.32	"	"	Parafield-Melbourne	7	25	
18.9.32	"	"	Melbourne-Wangaratta	2	15	Escorted Pilot Owen
21.9.32	"	"	Wang-Benalla		30	Collision Pilot Owen
21.9.32	"	"	Benalla-Wangaratta		20	
24.9.32	"	"	Wang-Goulbourn	5	5	
25.9.32	"	"	Goulbourn-Sydney	1	20	
25.9.32	"	"	Sydney-Newcastle	1	30	
27.9.32	"	"	Newcastle-Brisbane	4	00	

Mrs Bonney became the first woman to circumnavigate Australia by air. She was airborne for 95 hours and 27 minutes on her 12 800-kilometre flight.

APPENDIX 3

Details taken from Mrs Bonney's Pilot Log Book
Australia-England Flight 1933

DATE	AIRCRAFT Type	AIRCRAFT Reg	JOURNEY	Time in air Hrs	Time in air Mins	REMARKS
10.4.33	DH 60	VH-UPV	Brisbane-Charleville	4	40	Landed 1.10.
11.4.33	"	"	Charleville-Longreach-Cloncurry	3	10	
12.4.33	"	"	Cloncurry-Camooweal	3	35	
13.4.33	"	"	Camooweal-Darwin	8	00	
15.4.33	"	"	Darwin-Kupang	5	00	Fair. Hit land one hour before expected
16.4.33	"	"	Kupang-Bali	8	00	Headwind. Landed short of fuel trying Surabaya nonstop
17.4.33	"	"	Bali-Surabaya-Batavia	8	15	Nothing to report
18.4.33	"	"	Batavia-Singapore	7	45	
20.4.33	"	"	Singapore-Alor Star-Bang Biang Island	11	00	Forced down in storm
25.5.33	"	"	Calcutta-Allahabad	7	00	Fair
26.5.33	"	"	Allahabad-Jhansi-Jodhpur	9	00	Very difficult
27.5.33	"	"	Jodhpur-Karachi	6	00	Easy
2.6.33	"	"	Karachi-Jask-Bandar Abbas	9	40	Trying conditions Longest hop
3.6.33	"	"	B'Abbas-Bushire	8	10	Took 3½ hours to do 108 miles

DATE	AIRCRAFT Type	Reg	JOURNEY	Time in air Hrs	Mins	REMARKS
4.6.33	"	"	Bushire-Basra-Baghdad	8	10	Bad dust storms Basra-Baghdad
5.6.33	"	"	Baghdad-Aleppo-Adana	8	00	Easy except for mountains
7.6.33	"	"	Adana-Konya-Constantinople	7	20	Bad weather. Flew at 10 000 feet over summit
8.6.33	"	"	Constantinople-Plovdiv	8	10	After Plovdiv had to land due storms on mountains
10.6.33	"	"	Plovdiv-Sofia	1	10	10 000 foot mountains
11.6.33	"	"	Sofia-Budapest	3	45	Very good, threaded way through valleys
12.6.33	"	"	Budapest-Gmund	5	30	Easy but bad weather. Force landed
13.6.33	"	"	Gmund-Linz	2	00	Good
17.6.33	"	"	Linz-Wartzburg	5	00	Storms
18.6.33	"	"	Wurtzburg-Frankfurt	1	30	
20.6.33	"	"	Frankfurt-Cologne	2	05	
21.6.33	"	"	Cologne-Croydon	5	20	

Mrs Bonney became the first woman to fly from Ausralia to England. She was airborne for 157 hours and 15 minutes on her 20 000-kilometre flight.

APPENDIX 4

Details taken from Mrs Bonney's Pilot Log Book
Australia-South Africa Flight 1937

DATE	AIRCRAFT Type	AIRCRAFT Reg	JOURNEY	Time in air Hrs	Time in air Mins	REMARKS
9.4.37	Klemm	VH-UVE	Brisbane-Blackall	7	25	
10.4.37	"	"	Blackall-Camooweal	5	45	
11.4.37	"	"	Camooweal-Darwin	6	45	
13.4.37	"	"	Darwin-Kupang	4	30	Fair, haze, squalls
14.4.37	"	"	Kupang-Lombok	6	00	Haze bad
15.4.37	"	"	Lombok (returned)	3	15	Very bad storms
15.4.37	"	"	Lombok-Surabaya	3	15	Still bad
16.4.37	"	"	Surabaya-Batavia	4	50	Circled due storms
17.4.37	"	"	Batavia-Muntok [Bangka]	6	00	Landed due storms
19.4.37	"	"	Muntok-Singapore	3	30	Good
20.4.37	"	"	Singapore-Penang	4	20	
21.4.37	"	"	Penang-Alor Star		30	Tyre burst
22.4.37	"	"	Alor Star-Bangkok	6	30	Fair
25.4.37	"	"	Bangkok (returned)	3	00	Very bad storms
1.5.37	"	"	Bangkok-Tavoy	2	00	
1.5.37	"	"	Tavoy (returned)	1	30	Too bad to go on
2.5.37	"	"	Tavoy-Rangoon	4	15	Good weather
3.5.37	"	"	Rangoon-Akyab	3	45	Fair
4.5.37	"	"	Akyab-Calcutta	5	35	Returned. Cowling broken
5.5.37	"	"	Calcutta-Allahabad	5	00	Hot, low cloud, bad visibility
6.5.37	"	"	Allahabad-Agra	3	30	
8.5.37	"	"	Agra-Delhi	1	00	Very hot
14.5.37	"	"	Delhi-Jodhpur	4	00	Very hot
18.5.37	"	"	Jodhpur-Karachi	4	30	Hot
19.5.37	"	"	Karachi-Jask	6	30	Bad visibility. Dangerous winds and heat

DATE	AIRCRAFT Type	Reg	JOURNEY	Time in air Hrs	Mins	REMARKS
20.5.37	"	"	Jask-Bushire	7	00	Terrible
21.5.37	"	"	Bushire-Basra	4	15	Terrible
28.5.37	"	"	Basra-Baghdad	3	30	Good
30.5.37	"	"	Baghdad-Cairo	8	30	Good
7.6.37	"	"	Cairo-Luxor	4	50	Engine trouble leaving Cairo
9.6.37	"	"	Luxor-Wadi Halfa	3	00	Good
10.6.37	"	"	Wadi Halfa-Khartoum	5	10	
12.6.37	"	"	Khartoum-Malakal	5	15	
14.6.37	"	"	Malakal (returned)	3	00	Tail skid broke on landing
10.7.37	"	"	Khartoum-Malakal	5	30	30 mins looking at game
11.7.37	"	"	Malakal-Juba	4	30	
13.7.37	"	"	Juba-Kisumu	5	10	
15.7.37	"	"	Kisumu-Nairobi	2	20	Blind flying
26.7.37	"	"	Nairobi-Arusha	2	45	Good
28.7.37	"	"	Arusha-Dodoma	2	50	Good in spots
29.7.37	"	"	Dodoma (returned)	4	00	Lost way
30.7.37	"	"	Dodoma-Mbeya	3	50	Low cloud. Awful country
31.7.37	"	"	Mbeya-Mpika	3	15	Rough country
31.7.37	"	"	Mpika-Broken Hill	2	45	Rough. Bushfire
3.8.37	"	"	Broken Hill-Lusaka		45	
5.8.37	"	"	Lusaka-Livingstone	2	30	
8.8.37	"	"	Livingstone-Bulawayo	2	25	
10.8.37	"	"	Bulawayo-Zimbabwe	2	35	Circled ruins
11.8.37	"	"	Zimbabwe-Pietersburg-Pretoria	4	10	
14.8.37	"	"	Pretoria-Johannesburg		25	
16.8.37	"	"	Johannesburg-Kimberley	3	00	
18.8.37	"	"	Kimberley-Cape Town	6	20	Terrible over Hex Mountains

Mrs Bonney became the first person to link Australia and South Africa by air. She was airborne 210 hours and 45 minutes on her 29 088-kilometre flight.

Index